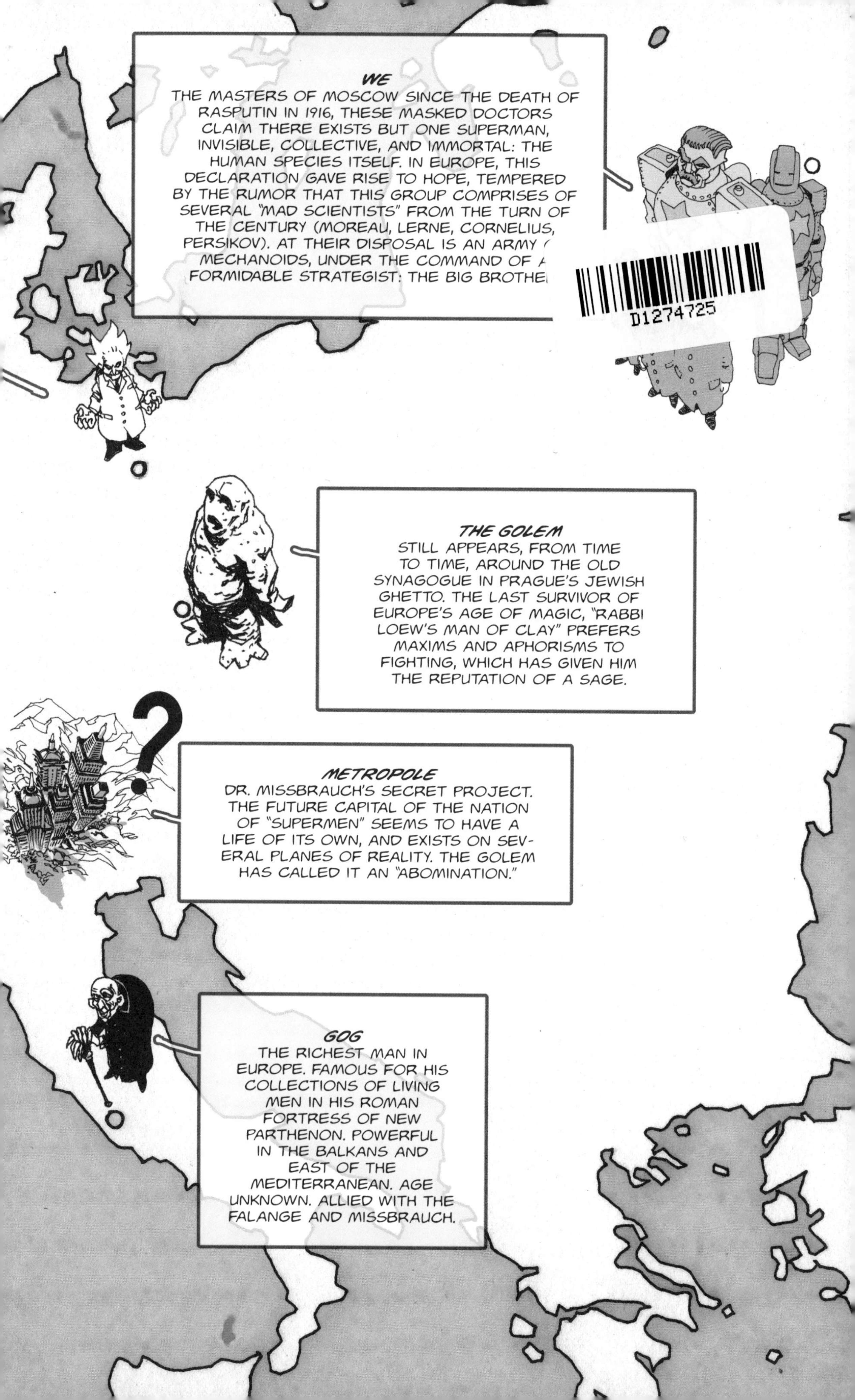
WE
THE MASTERS OF MOSCOW SINCE THE DEATH OF RASPUTIN IN 1916, THESE MASKED DOCTORS CLAIM THERE EXISTS BUT ONE SUPERMAN, INVISIBLE, COLLECTIVE, AND IMMORTAL: THE HUMAN SPECIES ITSELF. IN EUROPE, THIS DECLARATION GAVE RISE TO HOPE, TEMPERED BY THE RUMOR THAT THIS GROUP COMPRISES OF SEVERAL "MAD SCIENTISTS" FROM THE TURN OF THE CENTURY (MOREAU, LERNE, CORNELIUS, PERSIKOV). AT THEIR DISPOSAL IS AN ARMY
MECHANOIDS, UNDER THE COMMAND OF
FORMIDABLE STRATEGIST: THE BIG BROTHE
THE GOLEM
STILL APPEARS, FROM TIME TO TIME, AROUND THE OLD SYNAGOGUE IN PRAGUE'S JEWISH GHETTO. THE LAST SURVIVOR OF EUROPE'S AGE OF MAGIC, "RABBI LOEW'S MAN OF CLAY" PREFERS MAXIMS AND APHORISMS TO FIGHTING, WHICH HAS GIVEN HIM THE REPUTATION OF A SAGE.
METROPOLE
DR. MISSBRAUCH'S SECRET PROJECT. THE FUTURE CAPITAL OF THE NATION OF "SUPERMEN" SEEMS TO HAVE A LIFE OF ITS OWN, AND EXISTS ON SEVERAL PLANES OF REALITY. THE GOLEM HAS CALLED IT AN "ABOMINATION."
GOG
THE RICHEST MAN IN EUROPE. FAMOUS FOR HIS COLLECTIONS OF LIVING MEN IN HIS ROMAN FORTRESS OF NEW PARTHENON. POWERFUL IN THE BALKANS AND EAST OF THE MEDITERRANEAN. AGE UNKNOWN. ALLIED WITH THE FALANGE AND MISSBRAUCH.

THE CHIMERA BRIGADE

VOLUME 2

THE STORY SO FAR

In the trenches of World War I, a new generation of super-powered creatures was born - formed by new secret chemical weapons. Now, on the eve of another war, they have risen to take control of the capital cities of Europe.

In September 1938, invited by the sinister Dr Missbrauch, dozens of superhumans come to the newly established secret city of Metropole. The doctor offers them an alliance that will shift the balance of power in Europe and launch a war that will establish superpowered humans as the world's new master race. A scientist from the Radium Institute of Paris, Irène Joliot-Curie, secretly attends. The meeting is disrupted by the appearance of a strange visitor - a metamorph called Gregor Samsa, who then disappears under mysterious circumstances... Six months later, Irène and her husband, Frederic, employ the services of their old friend, The Man Who Walks Through Walls, to infiltrate the stronghold of the mighty Eye, the self-proclaimed protector of Paris, who they suspect is holding Gregor Samsa captive...

SERGE LEHMAN / FABRICE COLIN /
GESS / CELINE BESSONNEAU

THE CHIMERA BRIGADE

EPISODE TWO:
CAGLIOSTRO

EPISODE THREE:
THE BURNING CHAMBER

SCRIPT
SERGE LEHMAN
FABRICE COLIN

ART
GESS

COLORS
CELINE BESSONNEAU

TRANSLATION
EDWARD GAUVIN

LETTERING
GABRIELA HOUSTON

COVER
MAX BERTOLINI

WWW.TITAN-COMICS.COM
@COMICSTITAN
facebook.com/comicstitan

What did you think of this book?
We love to hear from our readers. Please email us at:
readercomments@titanemail.com,
or write to us at the above address.

Titan COMICS

CHIMERA BRIGADE VOLUME 2:
ISBN: 9781782761006

Collection Editor
Gabriela Houston

Collection Designer
Tom Hunt

Senior Editor
Steve White

Titan Comics Editorial
Andrew James, Tom Williams

Production Manager
Obi Onuora

Production Supervisor
Jackie Flook

Production Assistant
Peter James

Art Director
Oz Browne

Studio Manager
Emma Smith

Circulation Manager
Steve Tothill

Marketing Manager
Ricky Claydon

Senior Marketing and Press Executive
Owen Johnson

Publishing Manager
Darryl Tothill

Publishing Director
Chris Teather

Operations Director
Leigh Baulch

Executive Director
Vivian Cheung

Publisher
Nick Landau

Published by Titan Comics
A division of Titan Publishing Group Ltd.
144 Southwark St.
London, SE1 0UP

A CIP catalogue record for this title is available from the British Library.

First edition: April 2015

Originally published in 2009 by Librairie L'Atalante, France as La Brigade
Chimerique.

10 9 8 7 6 5 4 3 2 1

Printed in China. Titan Comics. TC0178

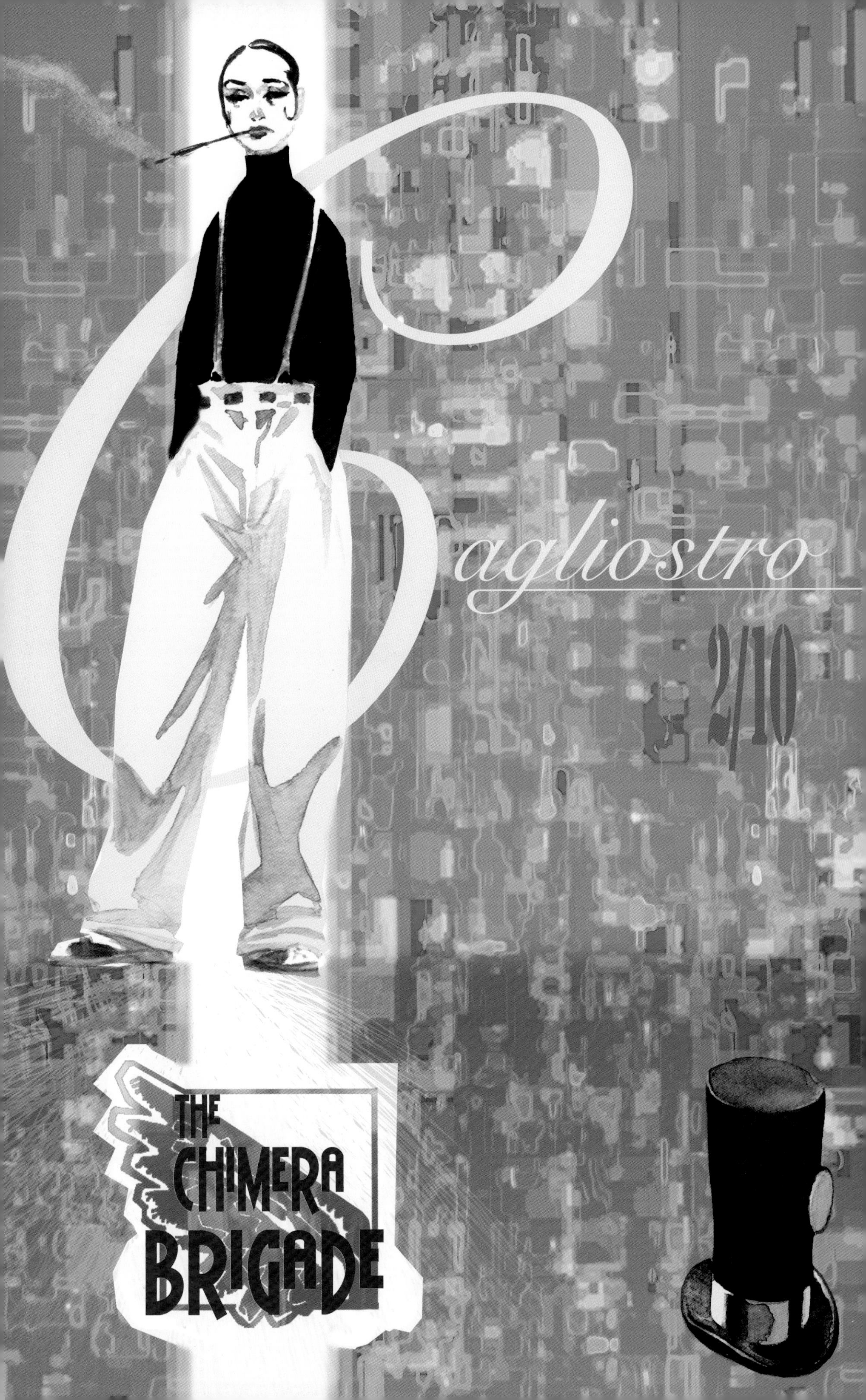
Cagliostro
2/10
THE CHIMERA BRIGADE

"Settle down, citizens. Help is on the way."

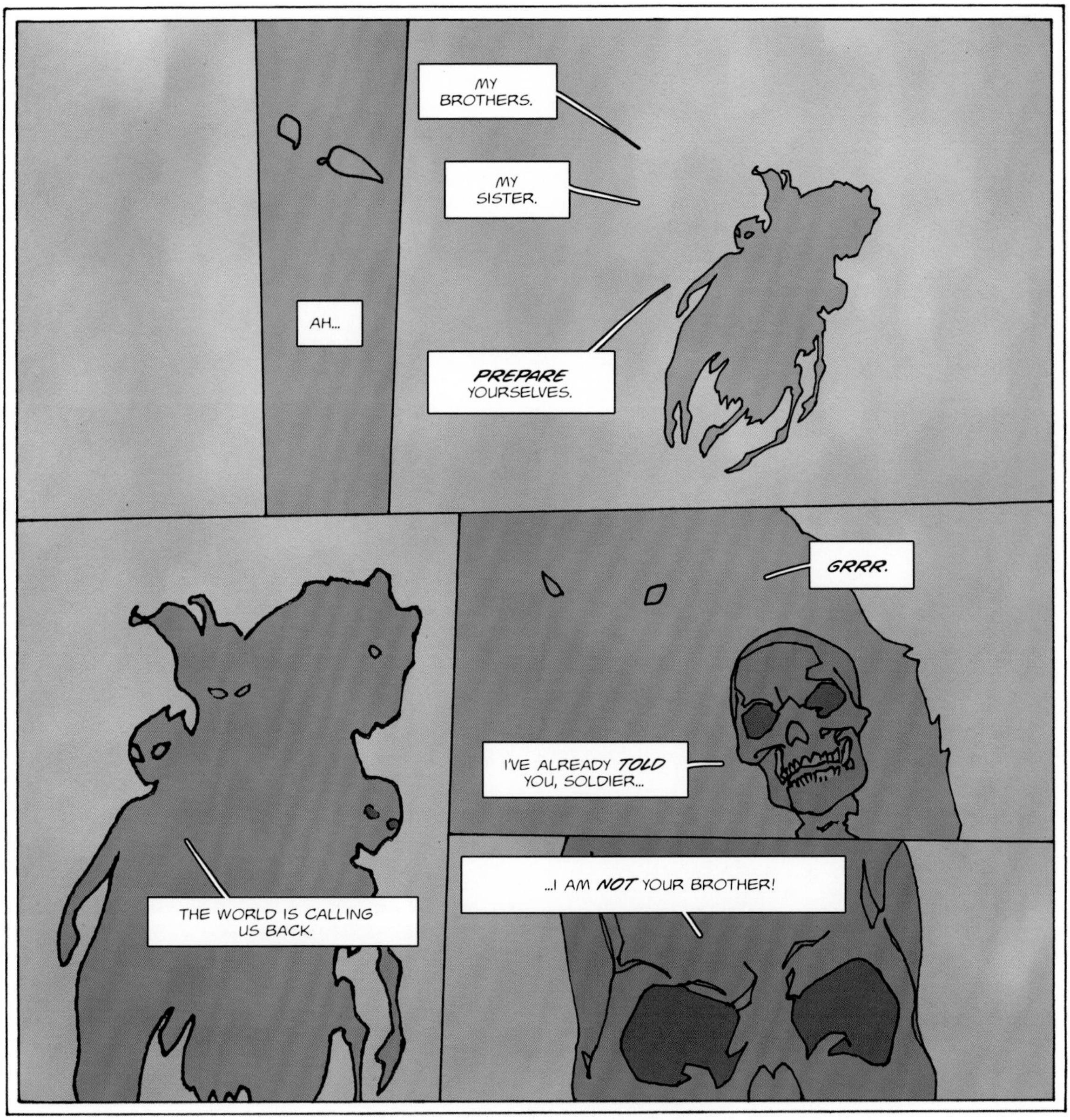
MY BROTHERS.
MY SISTER.
AH...
PREPARE YOURSELVES.
THE WORLD IS CALLING US BACK.
GRRR.
I'VE ALREADY TOLD YOU, SOLDIER...
...I AM NOT YOUR BROTHER!

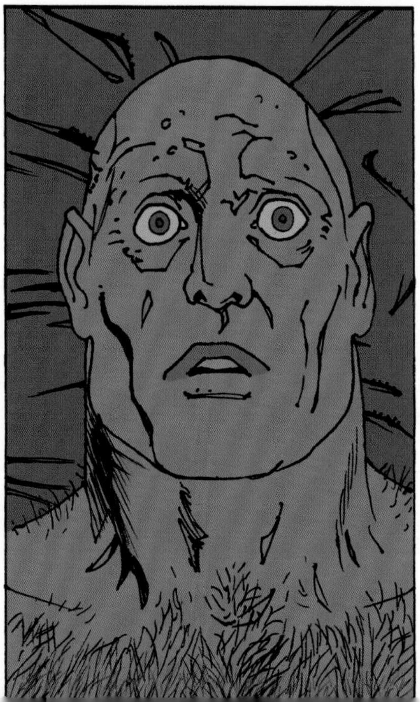

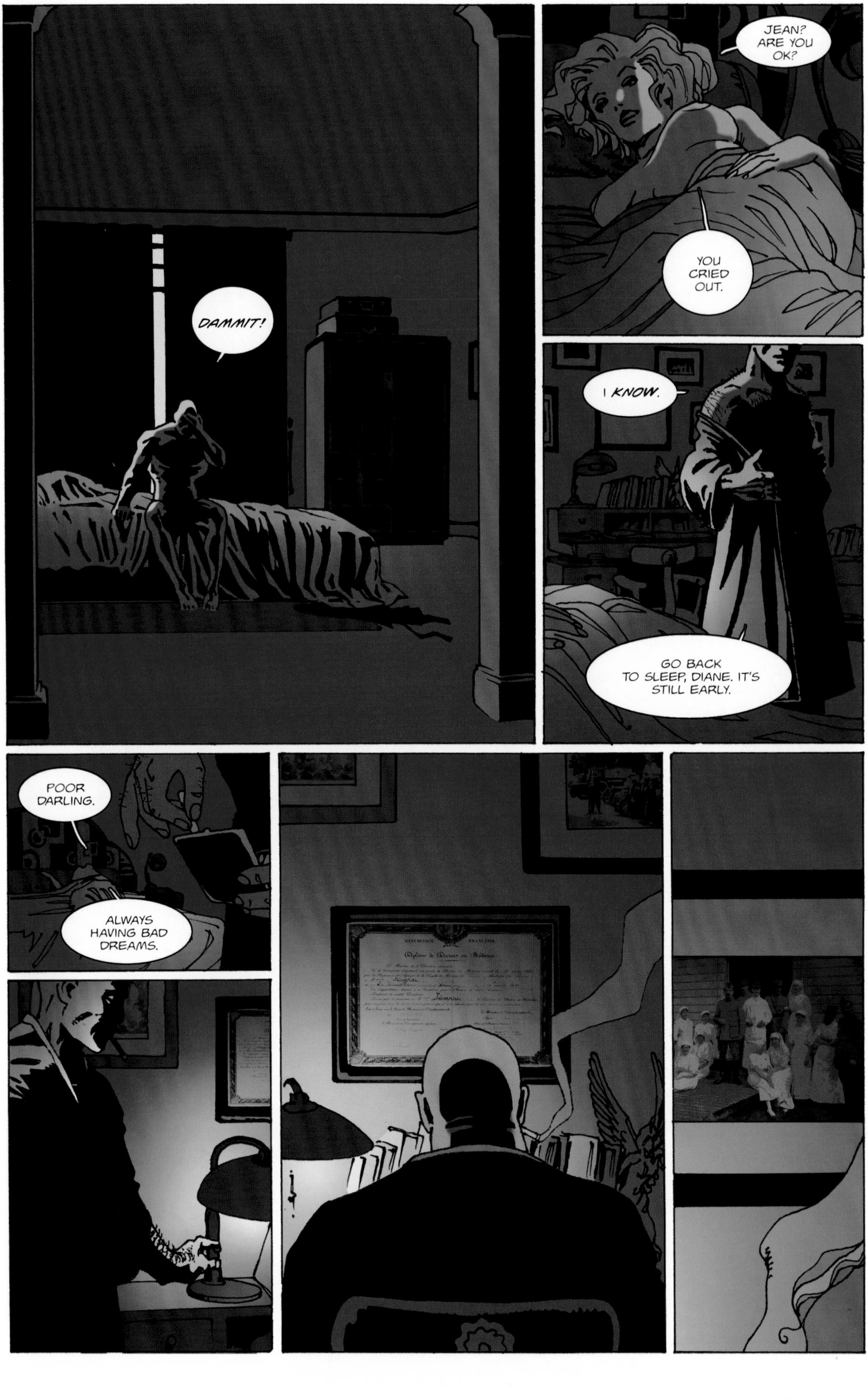
DAMMIT!
JEAN? ARE YOU OK?
YOU CRIED OUT.
I KNOW.
GO BACK TO SLEEP, DIANE. IT'S STILL EARLY.
POOR DARLING.
ALWAYS HAVING BAD DREAMS.

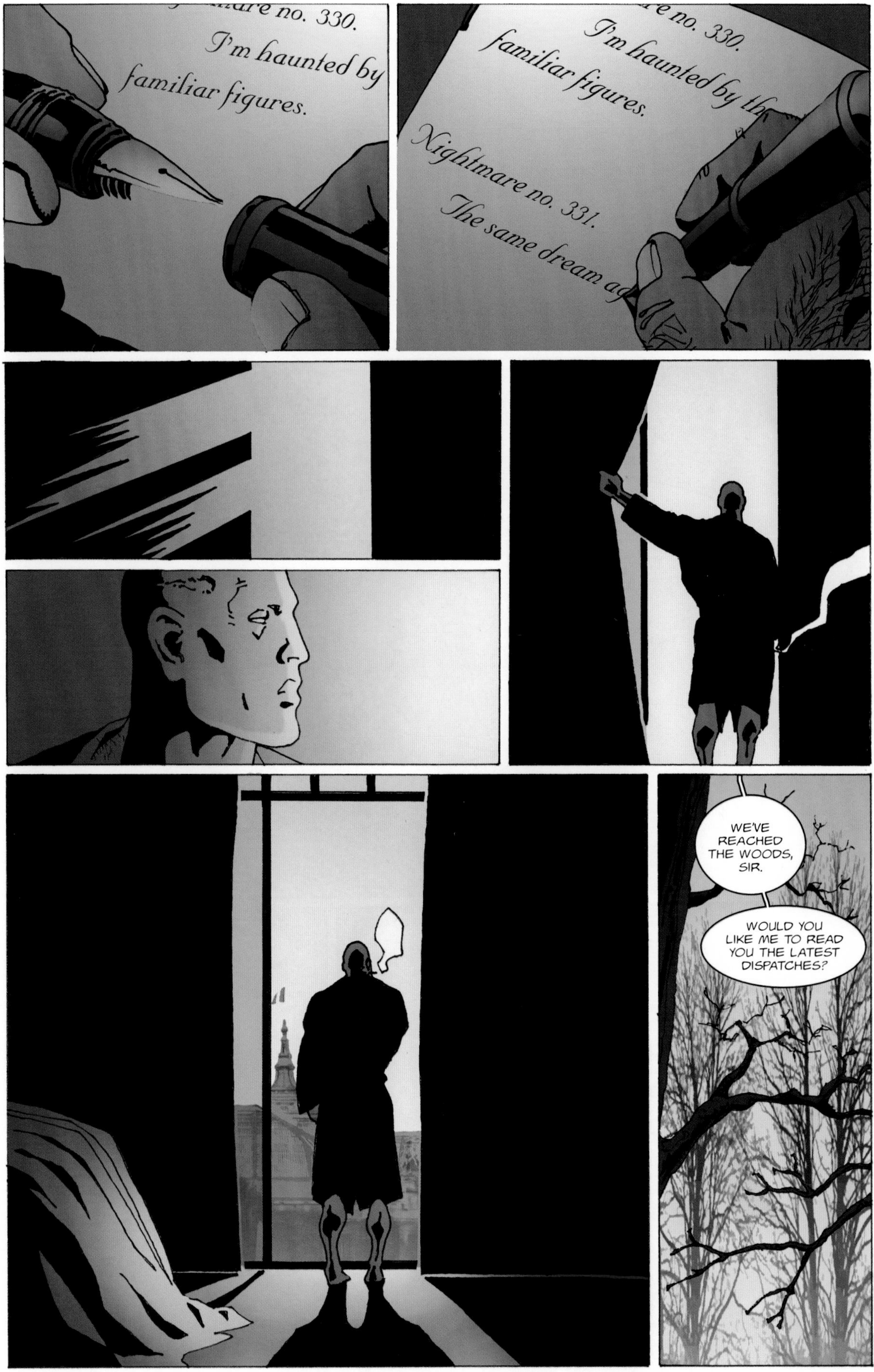
no. 330.
I'm haunted by
familiar figures.
no. 330.
I'm haunted by
familiar figures.
Nightmare no. 331.
The same dream
WE'VE REACHED THE WOODS, SIR.
WOULD YOU LIKE ME TO READ YOU THE LATEST DISPATCHES?

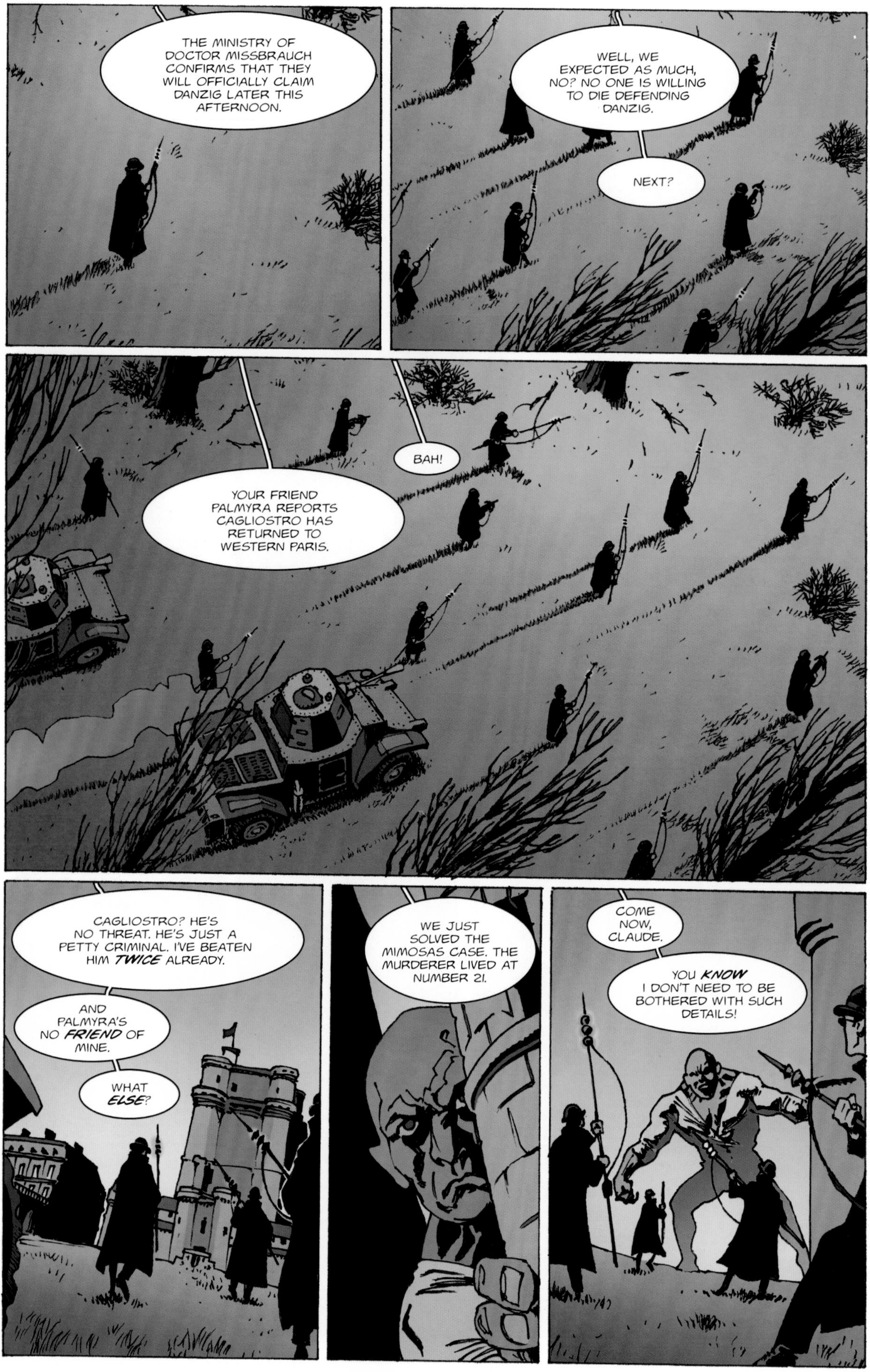
THE MINISTRY OF DOCTOR MISSBRAUCH CONFIRMS THAT THEY WILL OFFICIALLY CLAIM DANZIG LATER THIS AFTERNOON.
WELL, WE EXPECTED AS MUCH, NO? NO ONE IS WILLING TO DIE DEFENDING DANZIG.
NEXT?
BAH!
YOUR FRIEND PALMYRA REPORTS CAGLIOSTRO HAS RETURNED TO WESTERN PARIS.
CAGLIOSTRO? HE'S NO THREAT. HE'S JUST A PETTY CRIMINAL. I'VE BEATEN HIM TWICE ALREADY.
AND PALMYRA'S NO FRIEND OF MINE.
WHAT ELSE?
WE JUST SOLVED THE MIMOSAS CASE. THE MURDERER LIVED AT NUMBER 21.
COME NOW, CLAUDE.
YOU KNOW I DON'T NEED TO BE BOTHERED WITH SUCH DETAILS!

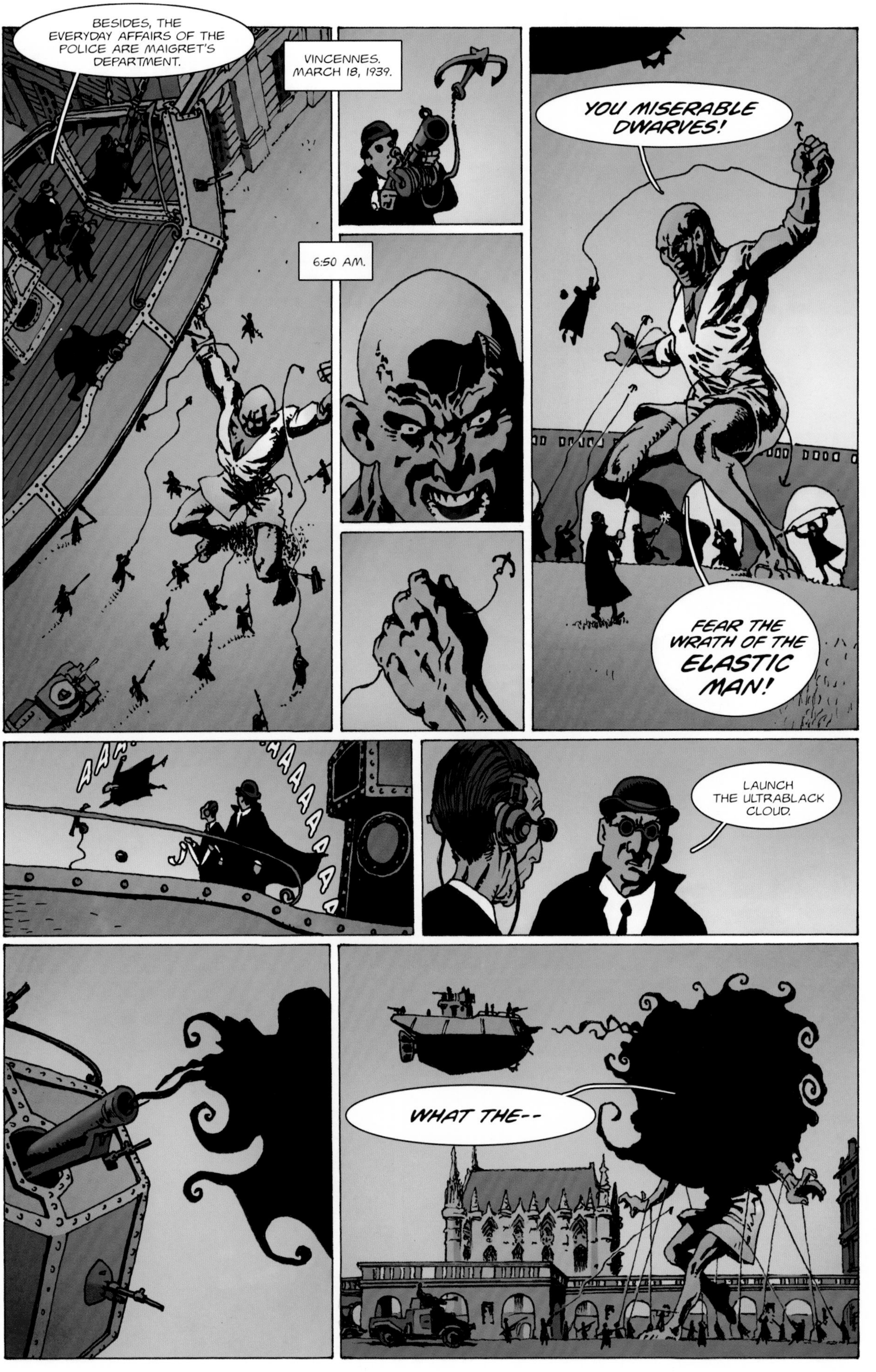
BESIDES, THE EVERYDAY AFFAIRS OF THE POLICE ARE MAIGRET'S DEPARTMENT.
VINCENNES. MARCH 18, 1939.
6:50 AM.
YOU MISERABLE DWARVES!
FEAR THE WRATH OF THE ELASTIC MAN!
LAUNCH THE ULTRABLACK CLOUD.
WHAT THE--

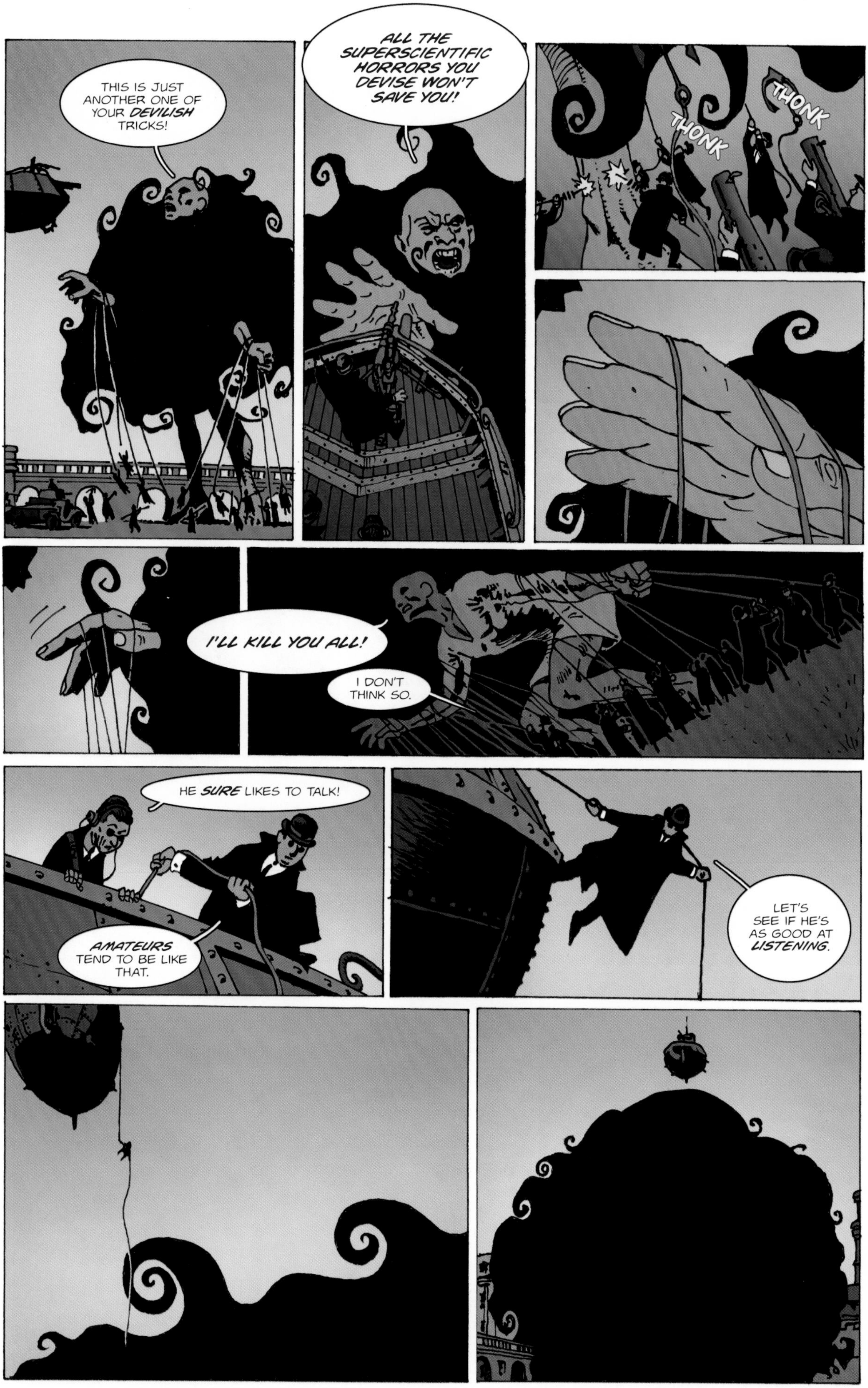
THIS IS JUST ANOTHER ONE OF YOUR DEVILISH TRICKS!
ALL THE SUPERSCIENTIFIC HORRORS YOU DEVISE WON'T SAVE YOU!
THONK
THONK
I'LL KILL YOU ALL!
I DON'T THINK SO.
HE SURE LIKES TO TALK!
AMATEURS TEND TO BE LIKE THAT.
LET'S SEE IF HE'S AS GOOD AT LISTENING.

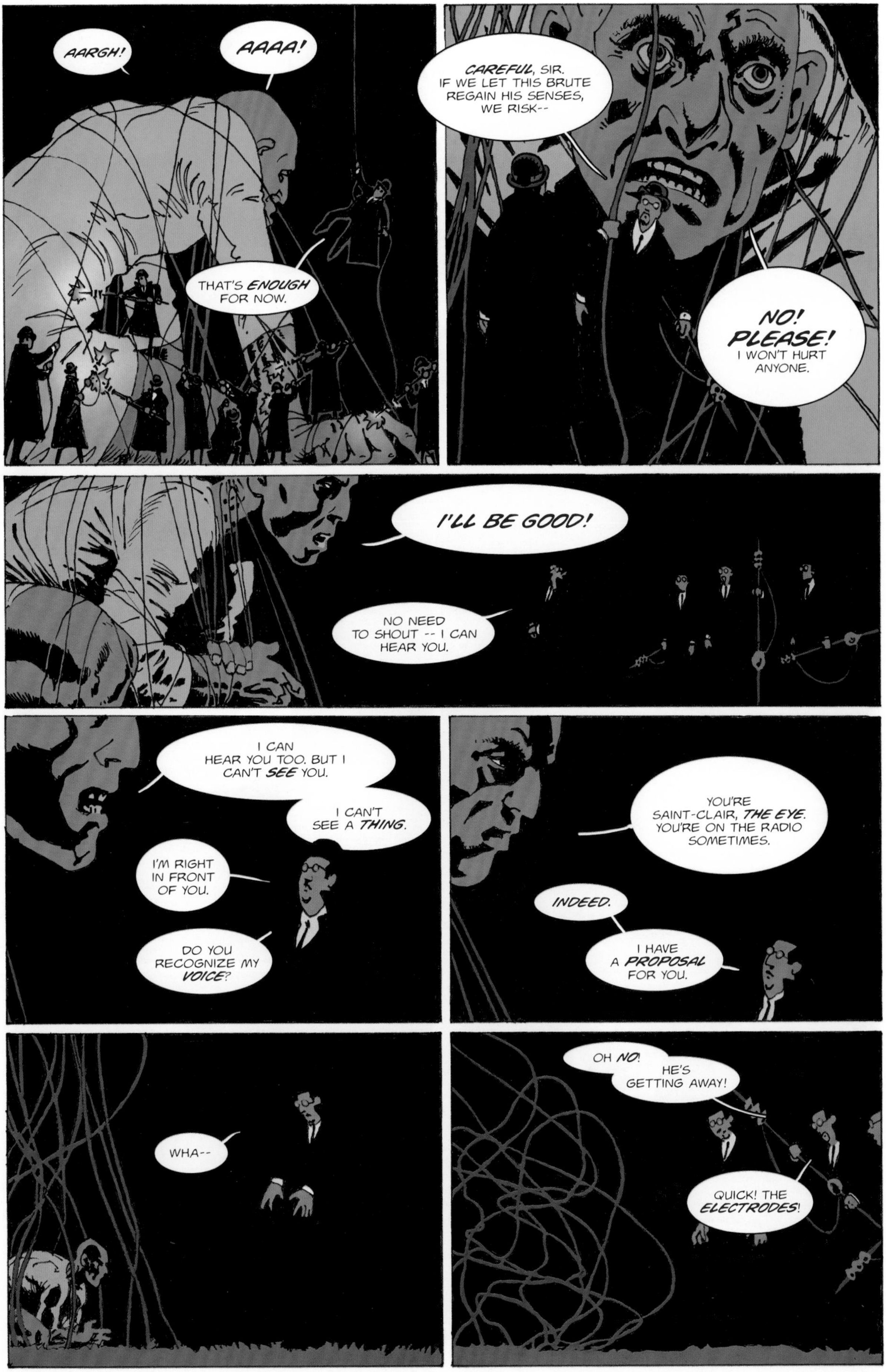
AARGH!
AAAA!
THAT'S ENOUGH FOR NOW.
CAREFUL, SIR. IF WE LET THIS BRUTE REGAIN HIS SENSES, WE RISK--
NO! PLEASE! I WON'T HURT ANYONE.
I'LL BE GOOD!
NO NEED TO SHOUT -- I CAN HEAR YOU.
I CAN HEAR YOU TOO. BUT I CAN'T SEE YOU.
I CAN'T SEE A THING.
I'M RIGHT IN FRONT OF YOU.
DO YOU RECOGNIZE MY VOICE?
YOU'RE SAINT-CLAIR, THE EYE. YOU'RE ON THE RADIO SOMETIMES.
INDEED.
I HAVE A PROPOSAL FOR YOU.
WHA--
OH NO! HE'S GETTING AWAY!
QUICK! THE ELECTRODES!

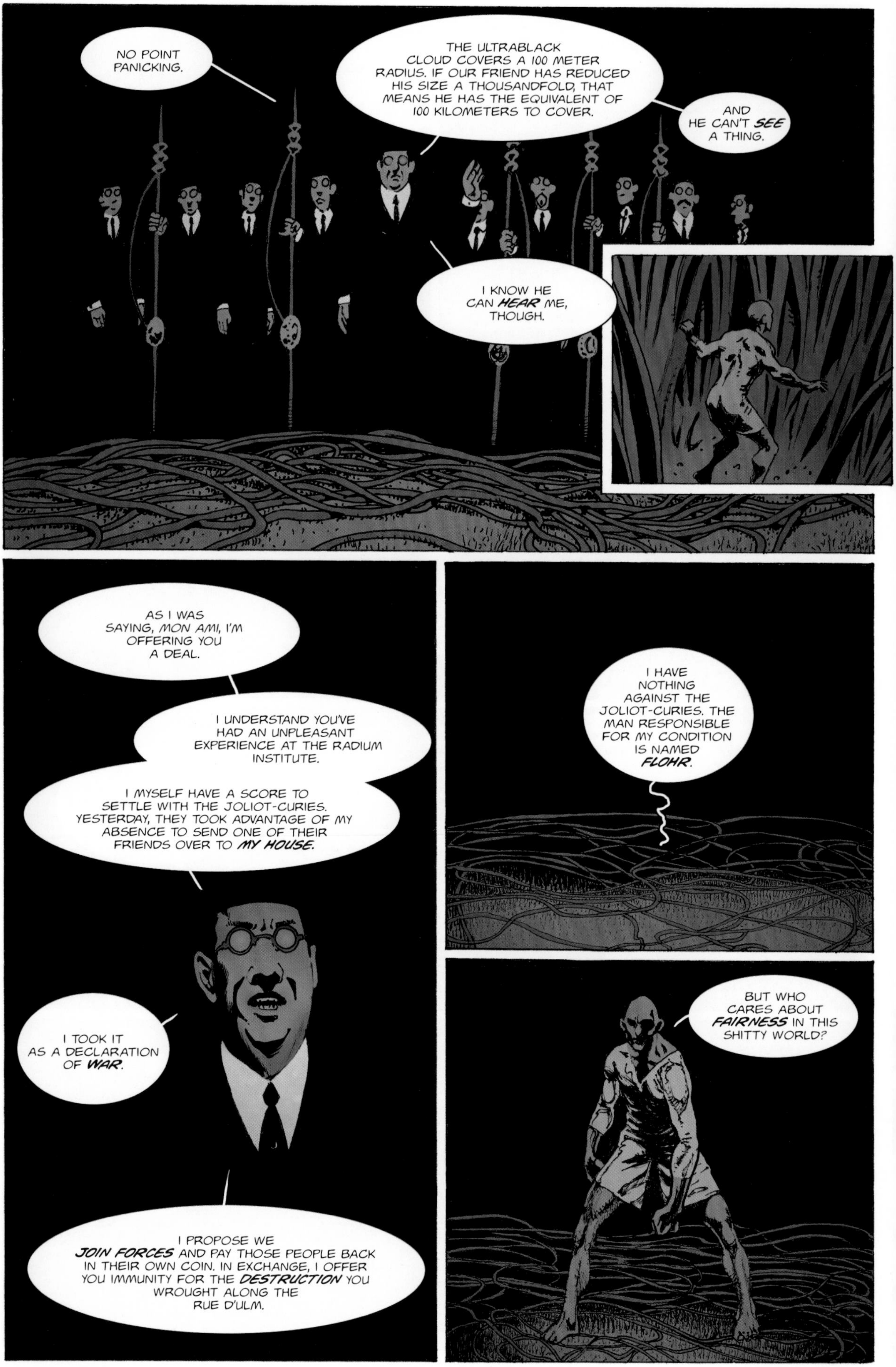

NO POINT PANICKING.
THE ULTRABLACK CLOUD COVERS A 100 METER RADIUS. IF OUR FRIEND HAS REDUCED HIS SIZE A THOUSANDFOLD, THAT MEANS HE HAS THE EQUIVALENT OF 100 KILOMETERS TO COVER.
AND HE CAN'T *SEE* A THING.
I KNOW HE CAN *HEAR* ME, THOUGH.
AS I WAS SAYING, *MON AMI*, I'M OFFERING YOU A DEAL.
I UNDERSTAND YOU'VE HAD AN UNPLEASANT EXPERIENCE AT THE RADIUM INSTITUTE.
I MYSELF HAVE A SCORE TO SETTLE WITH THE JOLIOT-CURIES. YESTERDAY, THEY TOOK ADVANTAGE OF MY ABSENCE TO SEND ONE OF THEIR FRIENDS OVER TO *MY HOUSE*.
I TOOK IT AS A DECLARATION OF *WAR*.
I PROPOSE WE *JOIN FORCES* AND PAY THOSE PEOPLE BACK IN THEIR OWN COIN. IN EXCHANGE, I OFFER YOU IMMUNITY FOR THE *DESTRUCTION* YOU WROUGHT ALONG THE RUE D'ULM.
I HAVE NOTHING AGAINST THE JOLIOT-CURIES. THE MAN RESPONSIBLE FOR MY CONDITION IS NAMED *FLOHR*.
BUT WHO CARES ABOUT *FAIRNESS* IN THIS SHITTY WORLD?

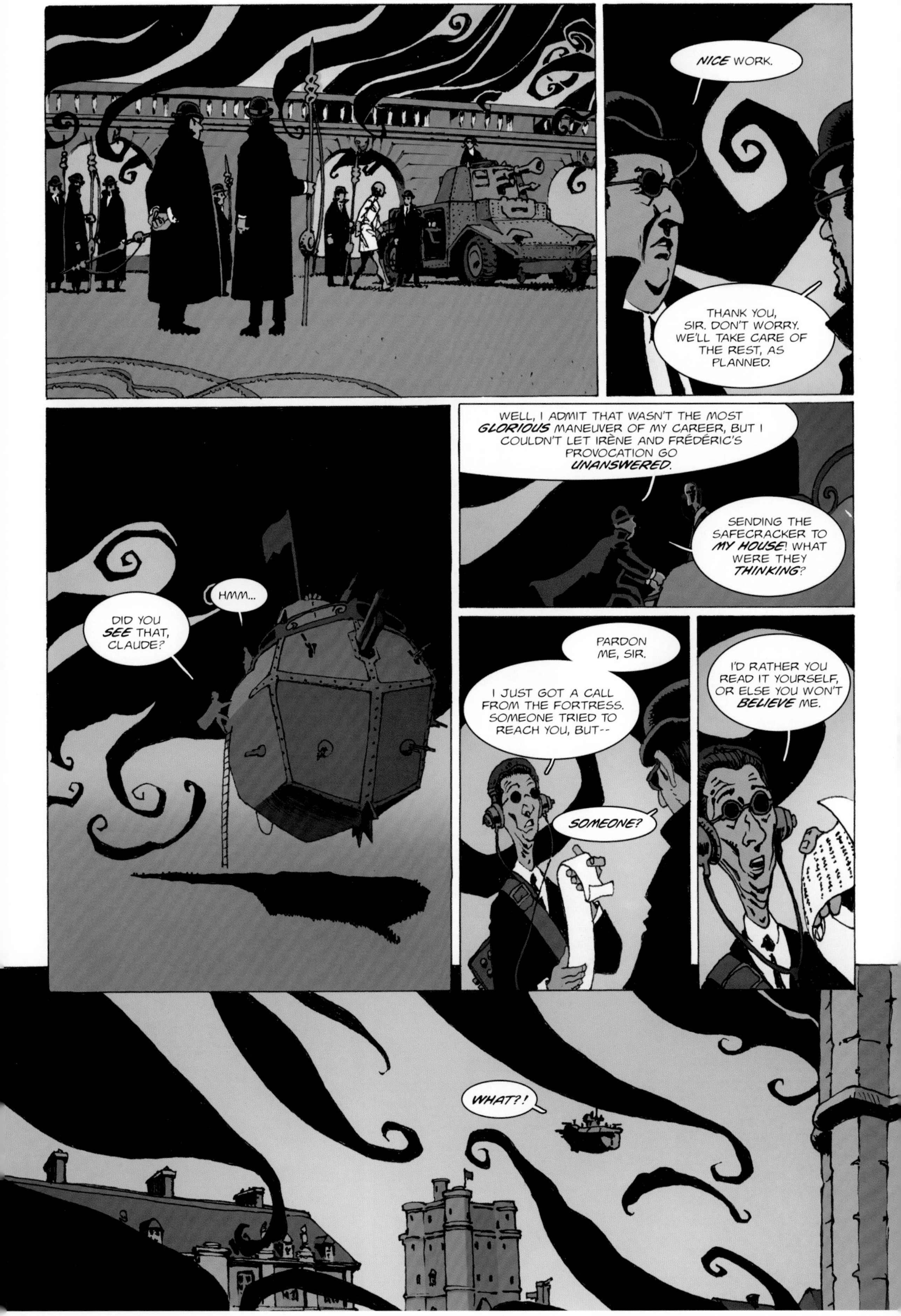
NICE WORK.
THANK YOU, SIR. DON'T WORRY. WE'LL TAKE CARE OF THE REST, AS PLANNED.
DID YOU SEE THAT, CLAUDE?
HMM...
WELL, I ADMIT THAT WASN'T THE MOST GLORIOUS MANEUVER OF MY CAREER, BUT I COULDN'T LET IRÈNE AND FRÉDÉRIC'S PROVOCATION GO UNANSWERED.
SENDING THE SAFECRACKER TO MY HOUSE! WHAT WERE THEY THINKING?
PARDON ME, SIR.
I JUST GOT A CALL FROM THE FORTRESS. SOMEONE TRIED TO REACH YOU, BUT--
SOMEONE?
I'D RATHER YOU READ IT YOURSELF, OR ELSE YOU WON'T BELIEVE ME.
WHAT?!

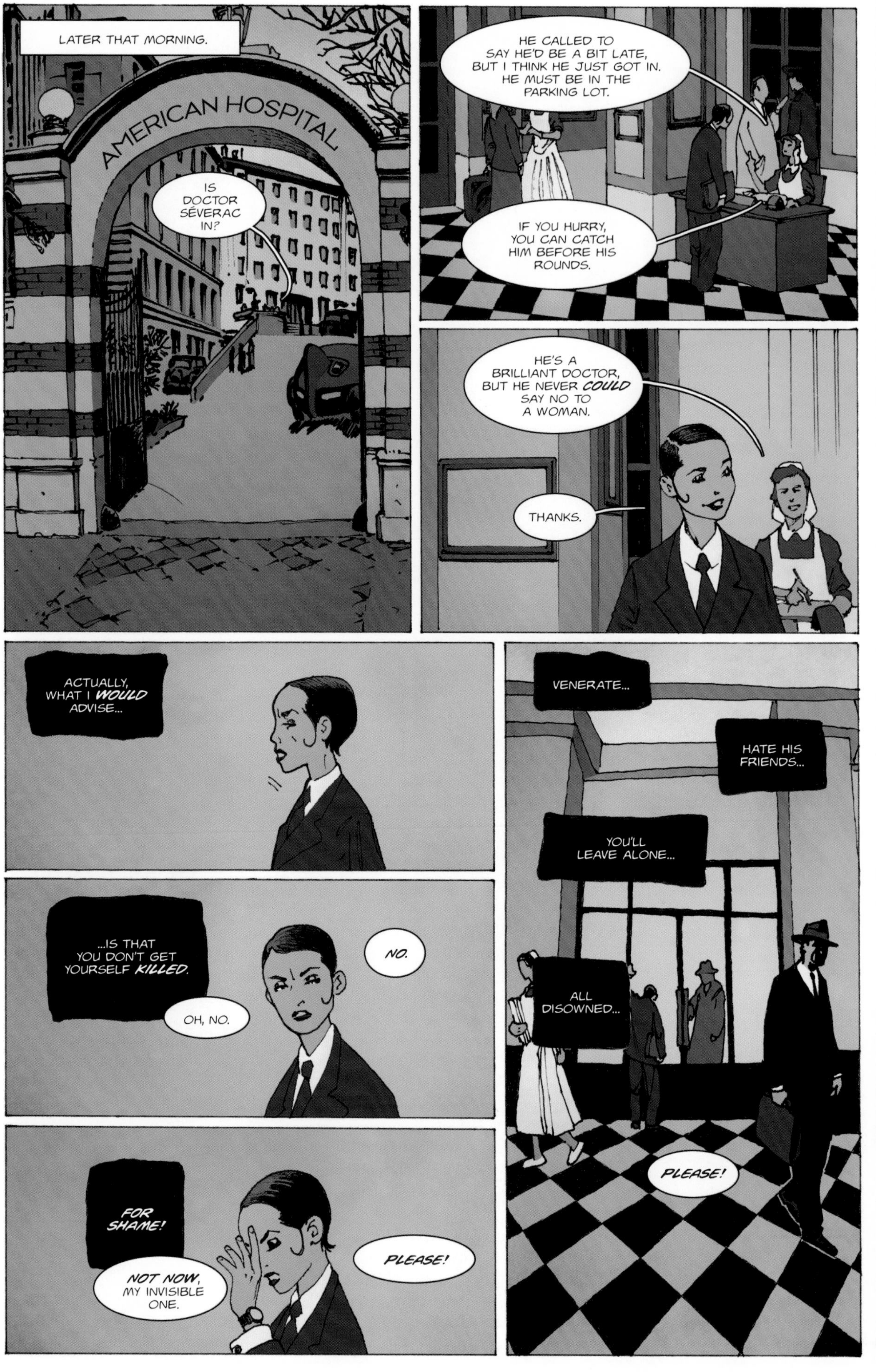
LATER THAT MORNING.
AMERICAN HOSPITAL
IS DOCTOR SÉVERAC IN?
HE CALLED TO SAY HE'D BE A BIT LATE, BUT I THINK HE JUST GOT IN. HE MUST BE IN THE PARKING LOT.
IF YOU HURRY, YOU CAN CATCH HIM BEFORE HIS ROUNDS.
HE'S A BRILLIANT DOCTOR, BUT HE NEVER COULD SAY NO TO A WOMAN.
THANKS.
ACTUALLY, WHAT I WOULD ADVISE...
...IS THAT YOU DON'T GET YOURSELF KILLED.
OH, NO.
NO.
FOR SHAME!
NOT NOW, MY INVISIBLE ONE.
PLEASE!
VENERATE...
HATE HIS FRIENDS...
YOU'LL LEAVE ALONE...
ALL DISOWNED...
PLEASE!

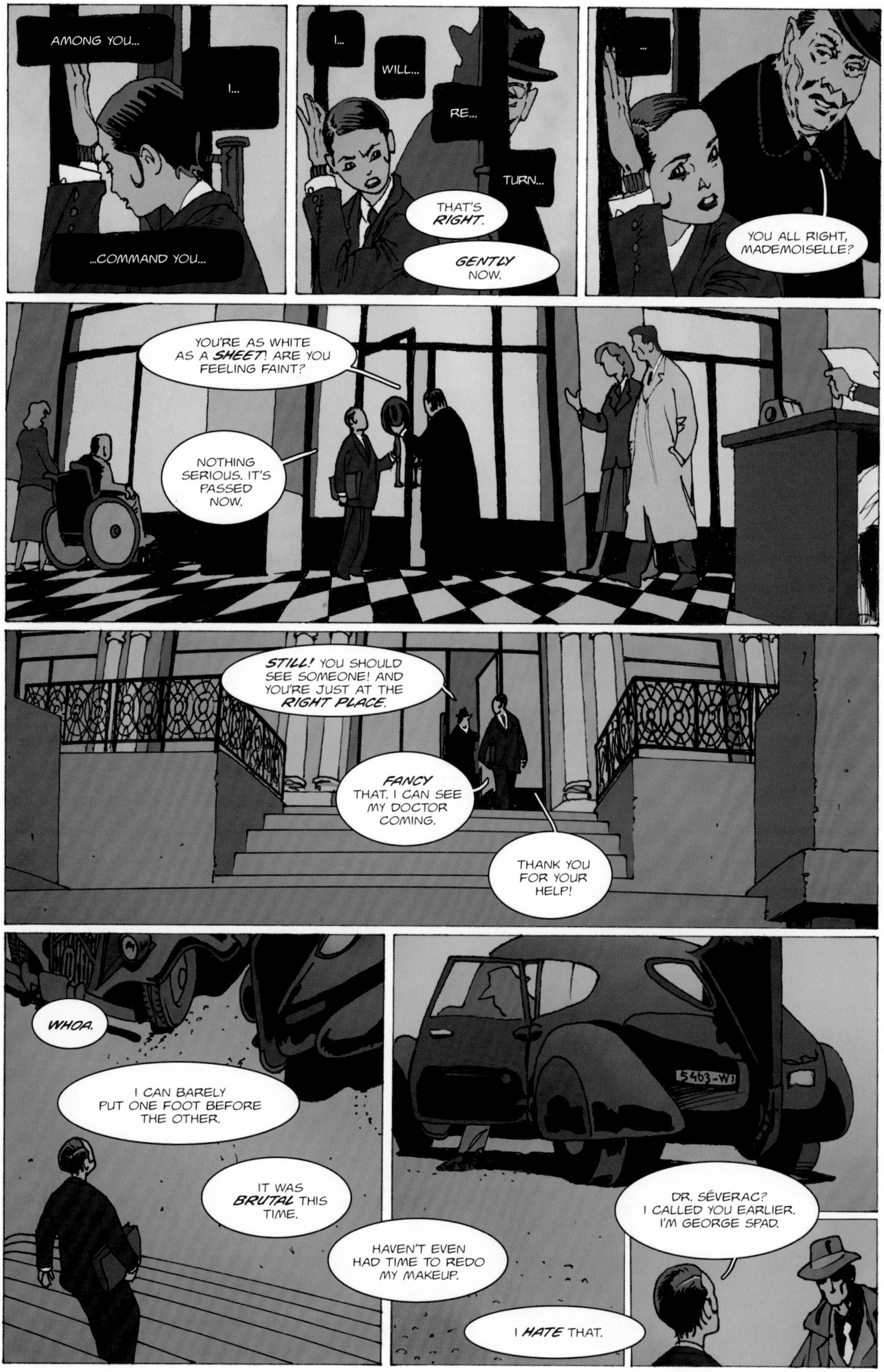
AMONG YOU...
I...
...COMMAND YOU...
I...
WILL...
RE...
TURN...
THAT'S *RIGHT*.
GENTLY NOW.
...
YOU ALL RIGHT, MADEMOISELLE?
YOU'RE AS WHITE AS A *SHEET*! ARE YOU FEELING FAINT?
NOTHING SERIOUS. IT'S PASSED NOW.
STILL! YOU SHOULD SEE SOMEONE! AND YOU'RE JUST AT THE *RIGHT PLACE*.
FANCY THAT. I CAN SEE MY DOCTOR COMING.
THANK YOU FOR YOUR HELP!
WHOA.
I CAN BARELY PUT ONE FOOT BEFORE THE OTHER.
IT WAS *BRUTAL* THIS TIME.
HAVEN'T EVEN HAD TIME TO REDO MY MAKEUP.
I *HATE* THAT.
DR. SÉVERAC? I CALLED YOU EARLIER. I'M GEORGE SPAD.

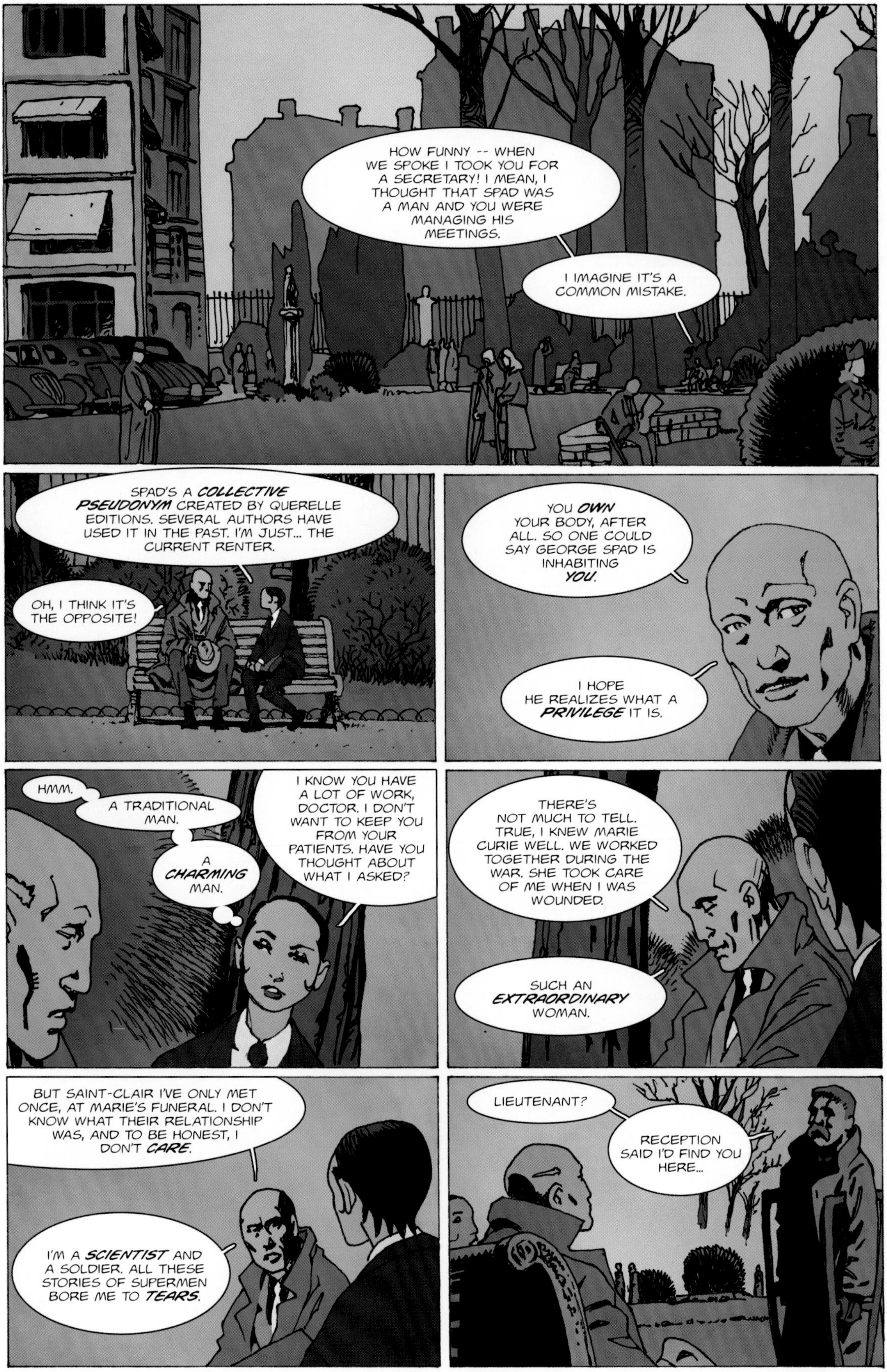
HOW FUNNY -- WHEN WE SPOKE I TOOK YOU FOR A SECRETARY! I MEAN, I THOUGHT THAT SPAD WAS A MAN AND YOU WERE MANAGING HIS MEETINGS.
I IMAGINE IT'S A COMMON MISTAKE.
SPAD'S A COLLECTIVE PSEUDONYM CREATED BY QUERELLE EDITIONS. SEVERAL AUTHORS HAVE USED IT IN THE PAST. I'M JUST... THE CURRENT RENTER.
OH, I THINK IT'S THE OPPOSITE!
YOU OWN YOUR BODY, AFTER ALL. SO ONE COULD SAY GEORGE SPAD IS INHABITING YOU.
I HOPE HE REALIZES WHAT A PRIVILEGE IT IS.
HMM.
A TRADITIONAL MAN.
A CHARMING MAN.
I KNOW YOU HAVE A LOT OF WORK, DOCTOR. I DON'T WANT TO KEEP YOU FROM YOUR PATIENTS. HAVE YOU THOUGHT ABOUT WHAT I ASKED?
THERE'S NOT MUCH TO TELL. TRUE, I KNEW MARIE CURIE WELL. WE WORKED TOGETHER DURING THE WAR. SHE TOOK CARE OF ME WHEN I WAS WOUNDED.
SUCH AN EXTRAORDINARY WOMAN.
BUT SAINT-CLAIR I'VE ONLY MET ONCE, AT MARIE'S FUNERAL. I DON'T KNOW WHAT THEIR RELATIONSHIP WAS, AND TO BE HONEST, I DON'T CARE.
I'M A SCIENTIST AND A SOLDIER. ALL THESE STORIES OF SUPERMEN BORE ME TO TEARS.
LIEUTENANT?
RECEPTION SAID I'D FIND YOU HERE...

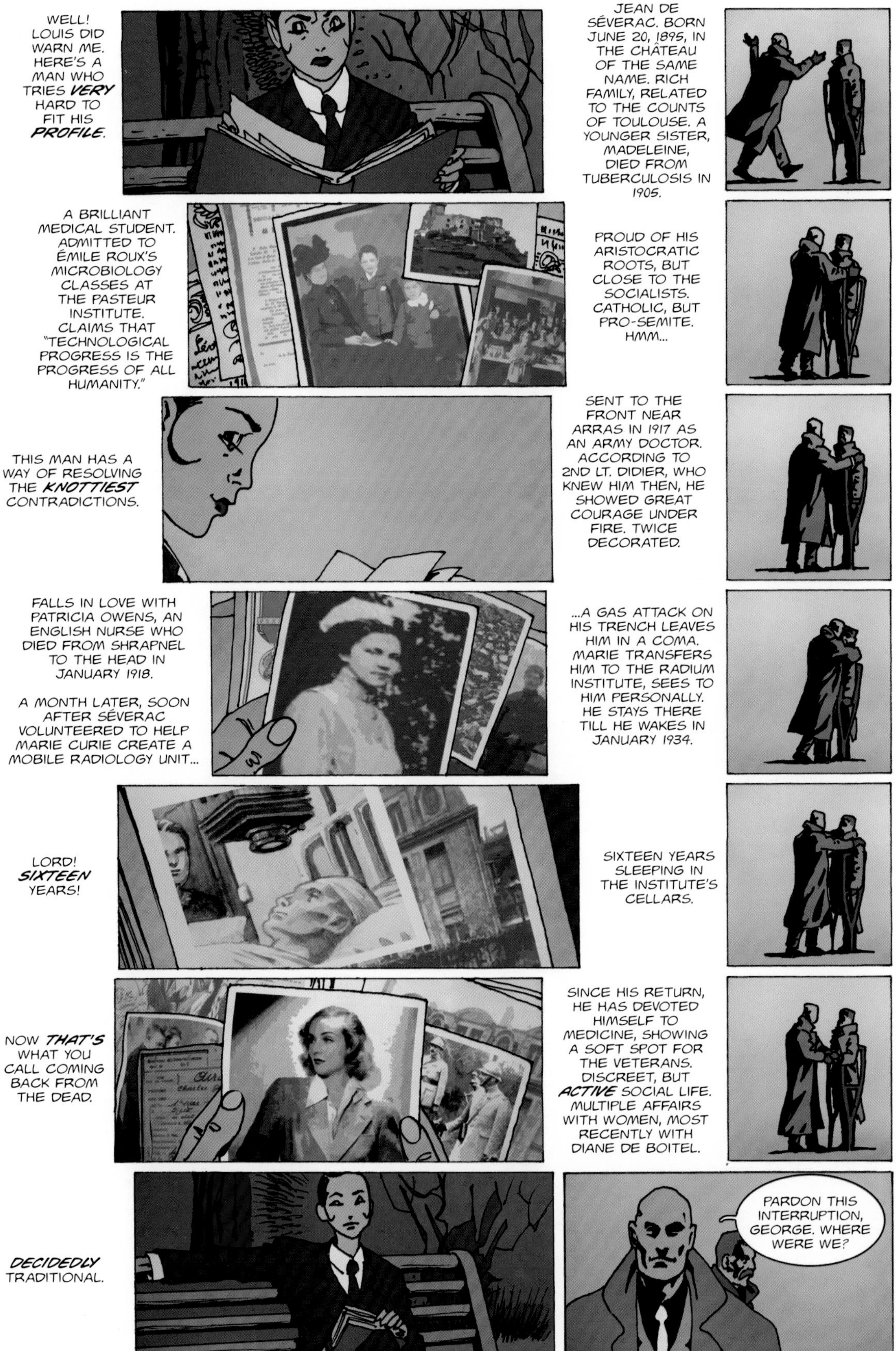
WELL! LOUIS DID WARN ME. HERE'S A MAN WHO TRIES *VERY* HARD TO FIT HIS *PROFILE*.
JEAN DE SÉVERAC. BORN JUNE 20, 1895, IN THE CHÂTEAU OF THE SAME NAME. RICH FAMILY, RELATED TO THE COUNTS OF TOULOUSE. A YOUNGER SISTER, MADELEINE, DIED FROM TUBERCULOSIS IN 1905.
A BRILLIANT MEDICAL STUDENT. ADMITTED TO ÉMILE ROUX'S MICROBIOLOGY CLASSES AT THE PASTEUR INSTITUTE. CLAIMS THAT "TECHNOLOGICAL PROGRESS IS THE PROGRESS OF ALL HUMANITY."
PROUD OF HIS ARISTOCRATIC ROOTS, BUT CLOSE TO THE SOCIALISTS. CATHOLIC, BUT PRO-SEMITE. HMM...
THIS MAN HAS A WAY OF RESOLVING THE *KNOTTIEST* CONTRADICTIONS.
SENT TO THE FRONT NEAR ARRAS IN 1917 AS AN ARMY DOCTOR. ACCORDING TO 2ND LT. DIDIER, WHO KNEW HIM THEN, HE SHOWED GREAT COURAGE UNDER FIRE. TWICE DECORATED.
FALLS IN LOVE WITH PATRICIA OWENS, AN ENGLISH NURSE WHO DIED FROM SHRAPNEL TO THE HEAD IN JANUARY 1918.
A MONTH LATER, SOON AFTER SÉVERAC VOLUNTEERED TO HELP MARIE CURIE CREATE A MOBILE RADIOLOGY UNIT...
...A GAS ATTACK ON HIS TRENCH LEAVES HIM IN A COMA. MARIE TRANSFERS HIM TO THE RADIUM INSTITUTE, SEES TO HIM PERSONALLY. HE STAYS THERE TILL HE WAKES IN JANUARY 1934.
LORD! *SIXTEEN* YEARS!
SIXTEEN YEARS SLEEPING IN THE INSTITUTE'S CELLARS.
NOW *THAT'S* WHAT YOU CALL COMING BACK FROM THE DEAD.
SINCE HIS RETURN, HE HAS DEVOTED HIMSELF TO MEDICINE, SHOWING A SOFT SPOT FOR THE VETERANS. DISCREET, BUT *ACTIVE* SOCIAL LIFE. MULTIPLE AFFAIRS WITH WOMEN, MOST RECENTLY WITH DIANE DE BOITEL.
DECIDEDLY TRADITIONAL.
PARDON THIS INTERRUPTION, GEORGE. WHERE WERE WE?

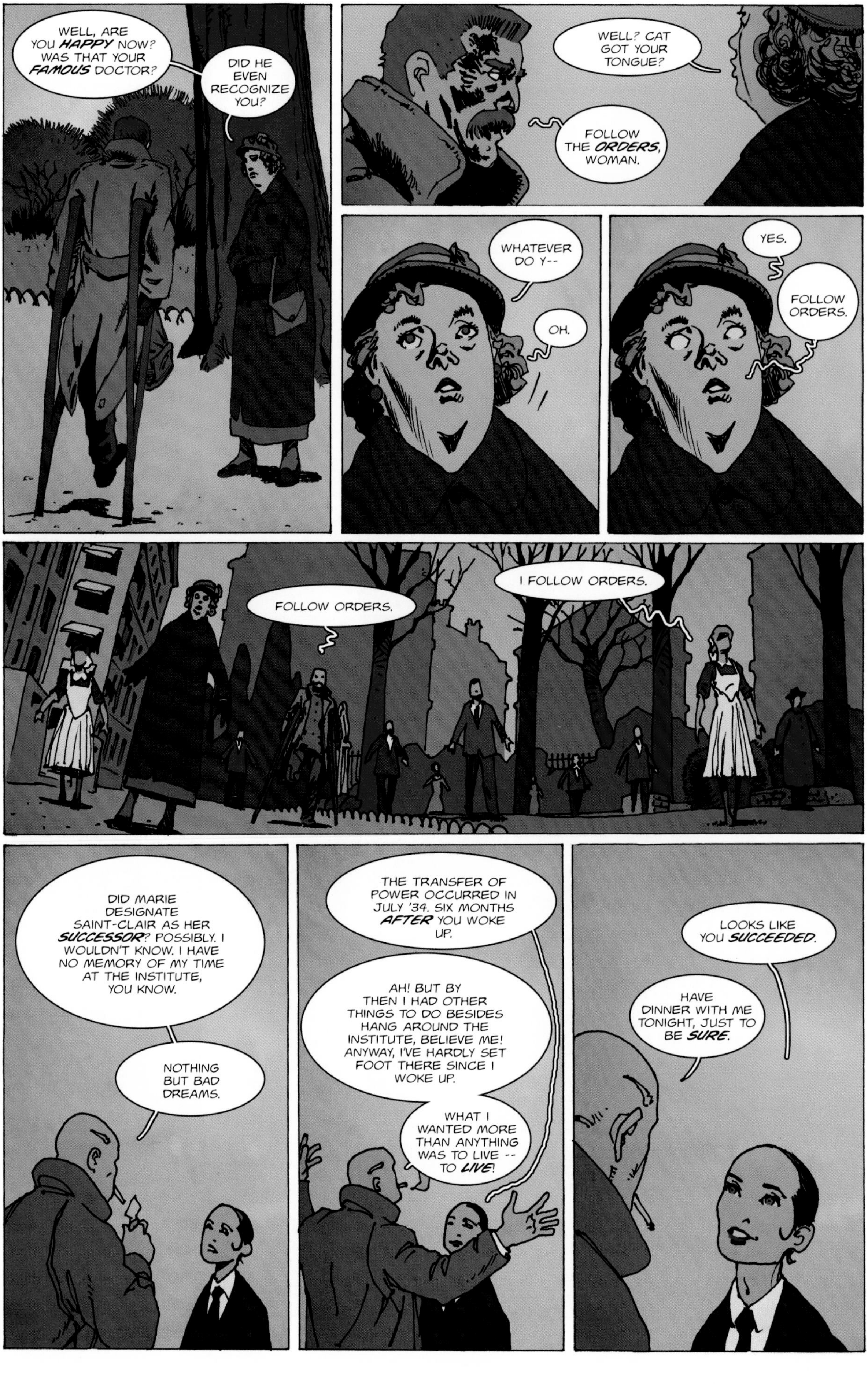
WELL, ARE YOU HAPPY NOW? WAS THAT YOUR FAMOUS DOCTOR?
DID HE EVEN RECOGNIZE YOU?
WELL? CAT GOT YOUR TONGUE?
FOLLOW THE ORDERS, WOMAN.
WHATEVER DO Y--
OH.
YES.
FOLLOW ORDERS.
FOLLOW ORDERS.
I FOLLOW ORDERS.
DID MARIE DESIGNATE SAINT-CLAIR AS HER SUCCESSOR? POSSIBLY. I WOULDN'T KNOW. I HAVE NO MEMORY OF MY TIME AT THE INSTITUTE, YOU KNOW.
NOTHING BUT BAD DREAMS.
THE TRANSFER OF POWER OCCURRED IN JULY '34. SIX MONTHS AFTER YOU WOKE UP.
AH! BUT BY THEN I HAD OTHER THINGS TO DO BESIDES HANG AROUND THE INSTITUTE, BELIEVE ME! ANYWAY, I'VE HARDLY SET FOOT THERE SINCE I WOKE UP.
WHAT I WANTED MORE THAN ANYTHING WAS TO LIVE -- TO LIVE!
LOOKS LIKE YOU SUCCEEDED.
HAVE DINNER WITH ME TONIGHT, JUST TO BE SURE.

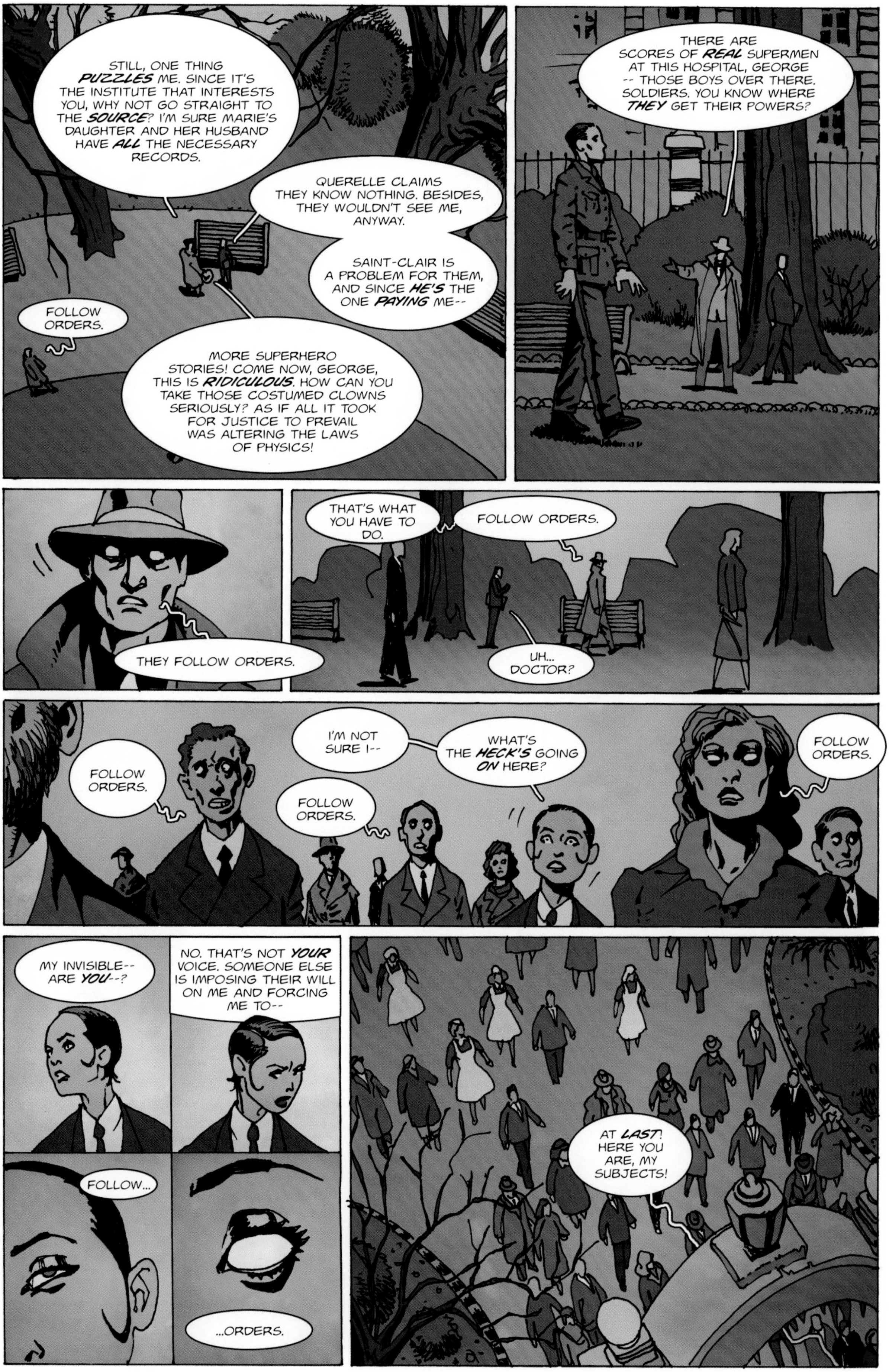
STILL, ONE THING PUZZLES ME. SINCE IT'S THE INSTITUTE THAT INTERESTS YOU, WHY NOT GO STRAIGHT TO THE SOURCE? I'M SURE MARIE'S DAUGHTER AND HER HUSBAND HAVE ALL THE NECESSARY RECORDS.
QUERELLE CLAIMS THEY KNOW NOTHING. BESIDES, THEY WOULDN'T SEE ME, ANYWAY.
SAINT-CLAIR IS A PROBLEM FOR THEM, AND SINCE HE'S THE ONE PAYING ME--
FOLLOW ORDERS.
MORE SUPERHERO STORIES! COME NOW, GEORGE, THIS IS RIDICULOUS. HOW CAN YOU TAKE THOSE COSTUMED CLOWNS SERIOUSLY? AS IF ALL IT TOOK FOR JUSTICE TO PREVAIL WAS ALTERING THE LAWS OF PHYSICS!
THERE ARE SCORES OF REAL SUPERMEN AT THIS HOSPITAL, GEORGE -- THOSE BOYS OVER THERE. SOLDIERS. YOU KNOW WHERE THEY GET THEIR POWERS?
THEY FOLLOW ORDERS.
THAT'S WHAT YOU HAVE TO DO.
FOLLOW ORDERS.
UH... DOCTOR?
FOLLOW ORDERS.
I'M NOT SURE I--
FOLLOW ORDERS.
WHAT'S THE HECK'S GOING ON HERE?
FOLLOW ORDERS.
MY INVISIBLE-- ARE YOU--?
NO. THAT'S NOT YOUR VOICE. SOMEONE ELSE IS IMPOSING THEIR WILL ON ME AND FORCING ME TO--
FOLLOW...
...ORDERS.
AT LAST! HERE YOU ARE, MY SUBJECTS!

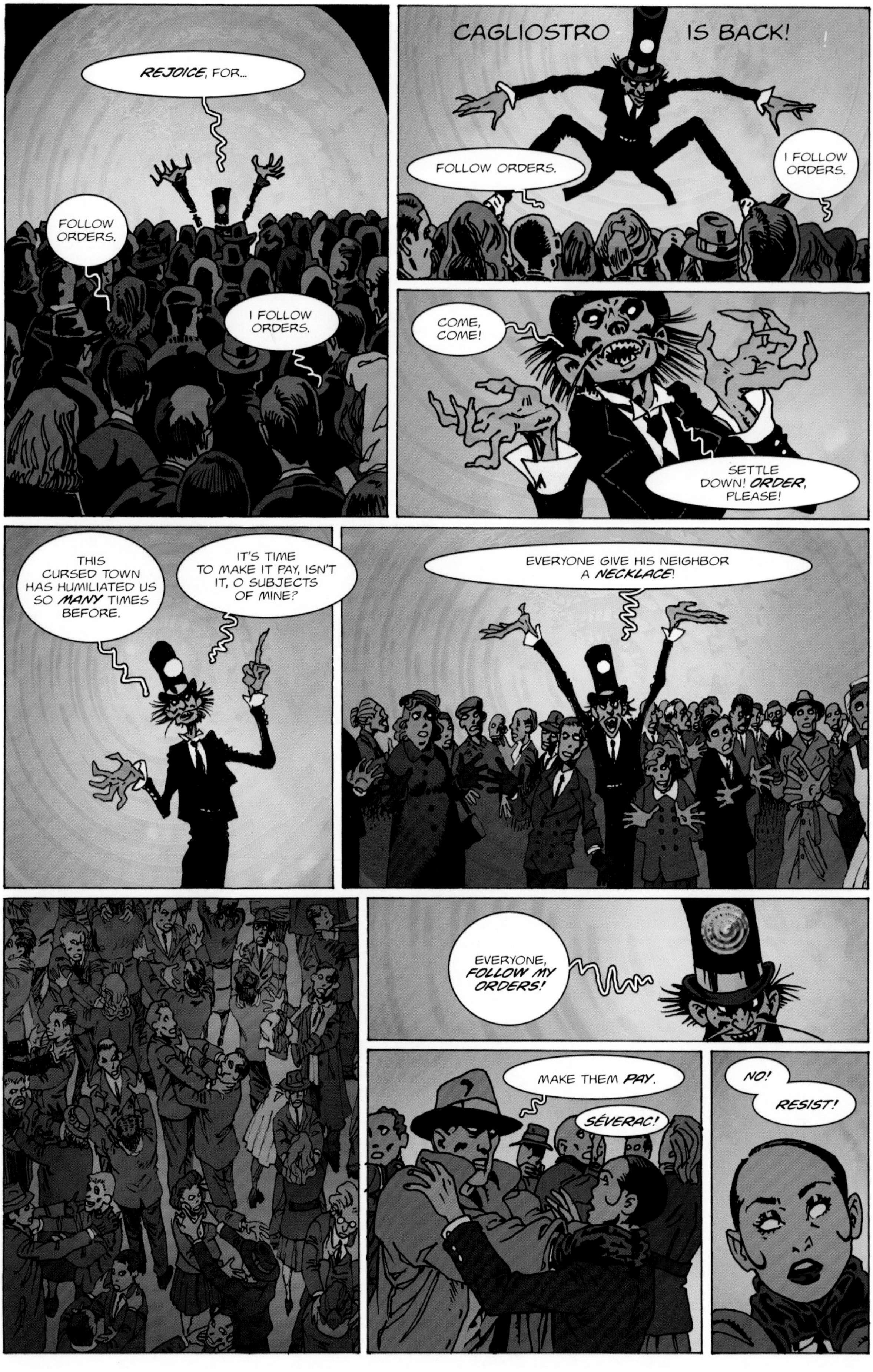
REJOICE, FOR...
FOLLOW ORDERS.
I FOLLOW ORDERS.
CAGLIOSTRO IS BACK!
FOLLOW ORDERS.
I FOLLOW ORDERS.
COME, COME!
SETTLE DOWN! ORDER, PLEASE!
THIS CURSED TOWN HAS HUMILIATED US SO MANY TIMES BEFORE.
IT'S TIME TO MAKE IT PAY, ISN'T IT, O SUBJECTS OF MINE?
EVERYONE GIVE HIS NEIGHBOR A NECKLACE!
EVERYONE, FOLLOW MY ORDERS!
MAKE THEM PAY.
SÉVERAC!
NO!
RESIST!

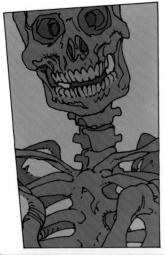

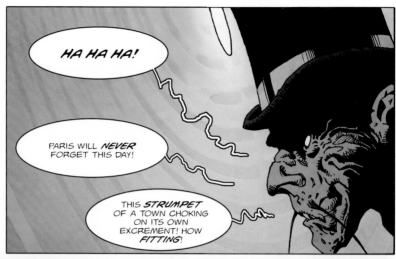

HA HA HA!

PARIS WILL *NEVER* FORGET THIS DAY!

THIS *STRUMPET* OF A TOWN CHOKING ON ITS OWN EXCREMENT! HOW *FITTING*!

HOLY SEPULCHER!

SUBJECTS! YOUR KING HAS BEEN INSULTED! *ILL-TREATED*! HIS NAME TAKEN IN VAIN!

WILL YOU *TOLERATE* THIS OUTRAGE?

HOW MANY *TIMES* MUST I *TELL* YOU, JOSEPH?

THE GOTHIC WAS ALREADY *PASSÉ* IN 1800.

THE WITCH!

CHARGE THE WITCH!

KILL!

KILL!

BURN THE WITCH!

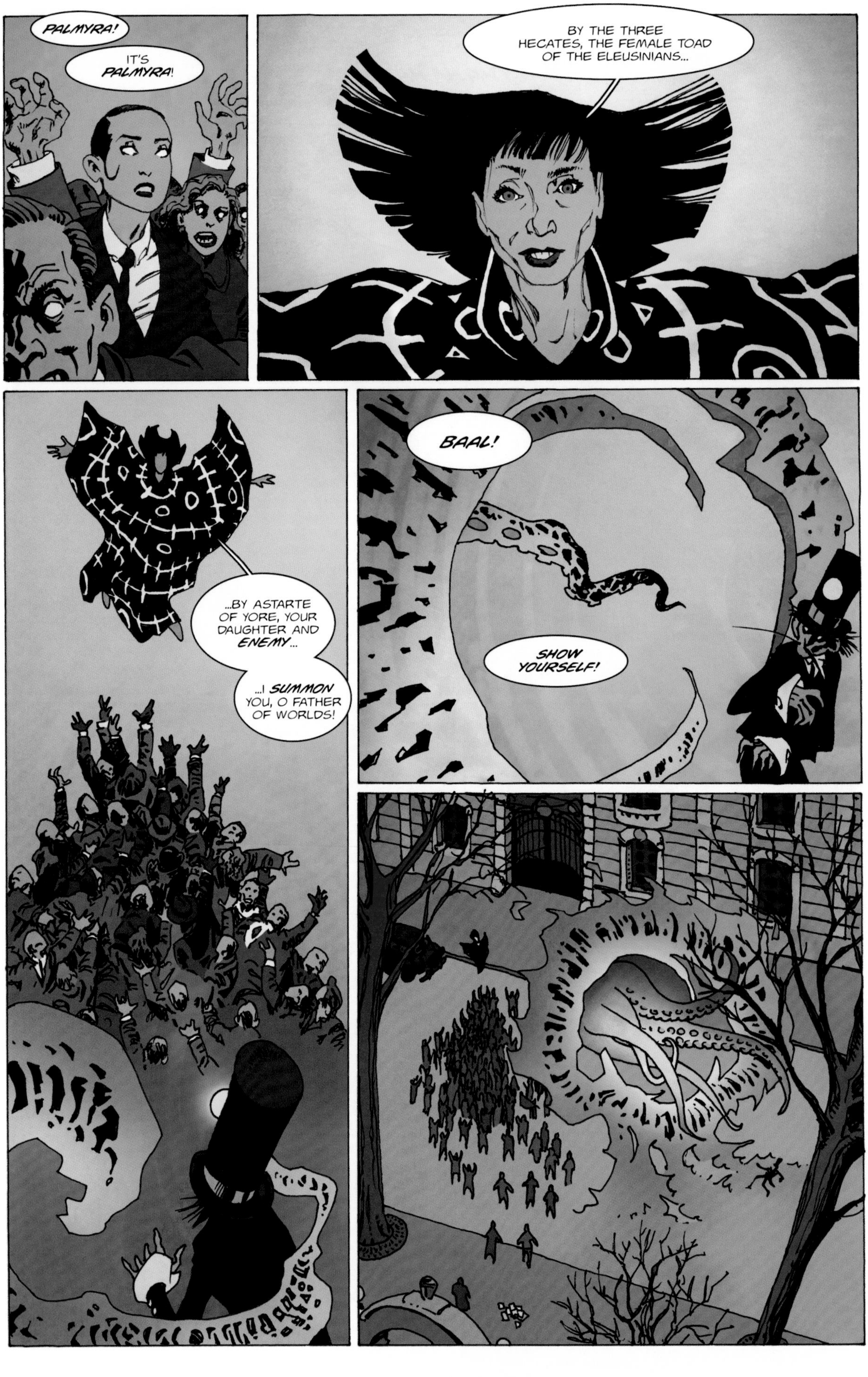
PALMYRA!
IT'S PALMYRA!
BY THE THREE HECATES, THE FEMALE TOAD OF THE ELEUSINIANS...
...BY ASTARTE OF YORE, YOUR DAUGHTER AND ENEMY...
...I SUMMON YOU, O FATHER OF WORLDS!
BAAL!
SHOW YOURSELF!

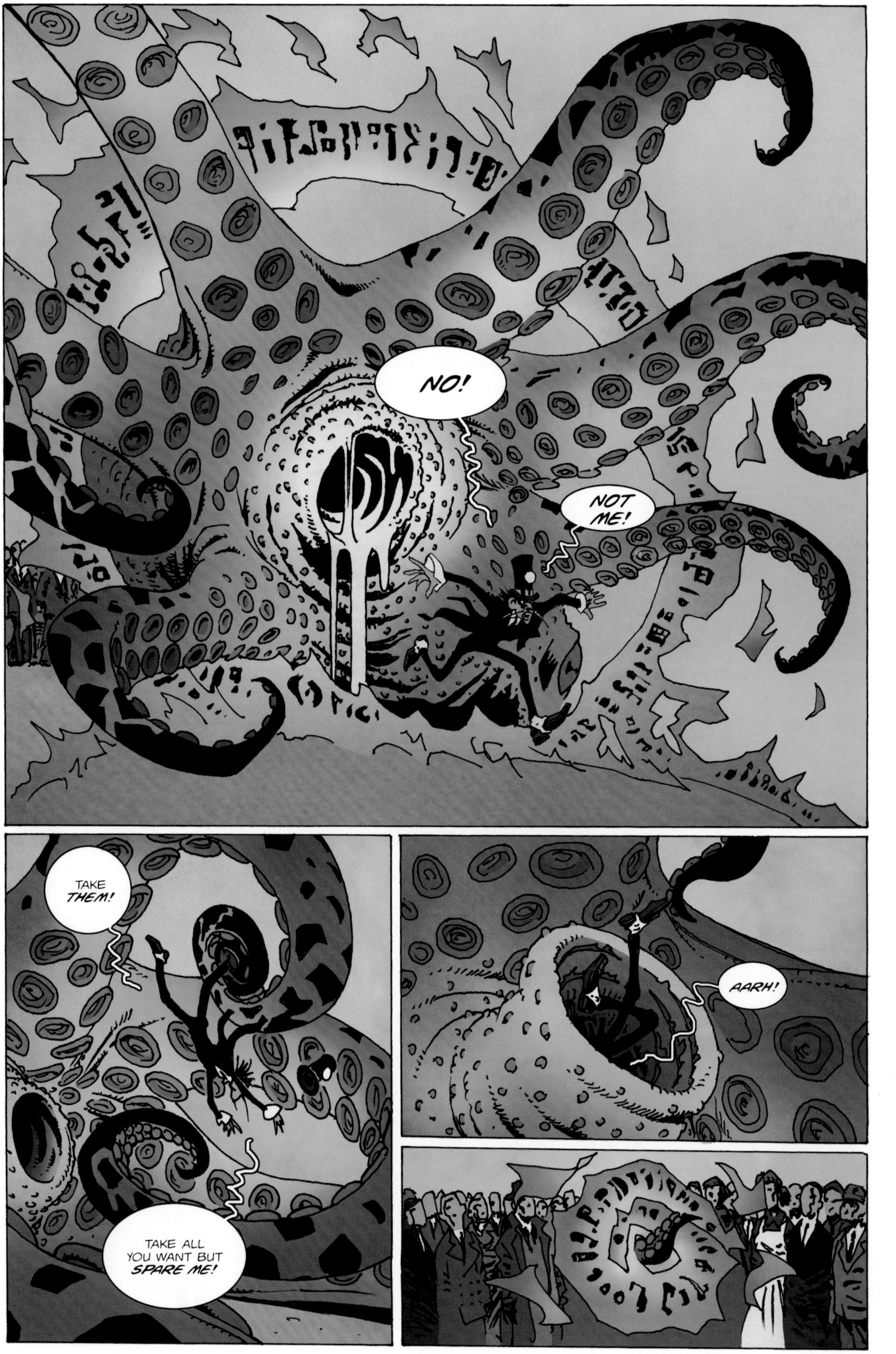
NO!
NOT ME!
TAKE THEM!
TAKE ALL YOU WANT BUT SPARE ME!
AARH!

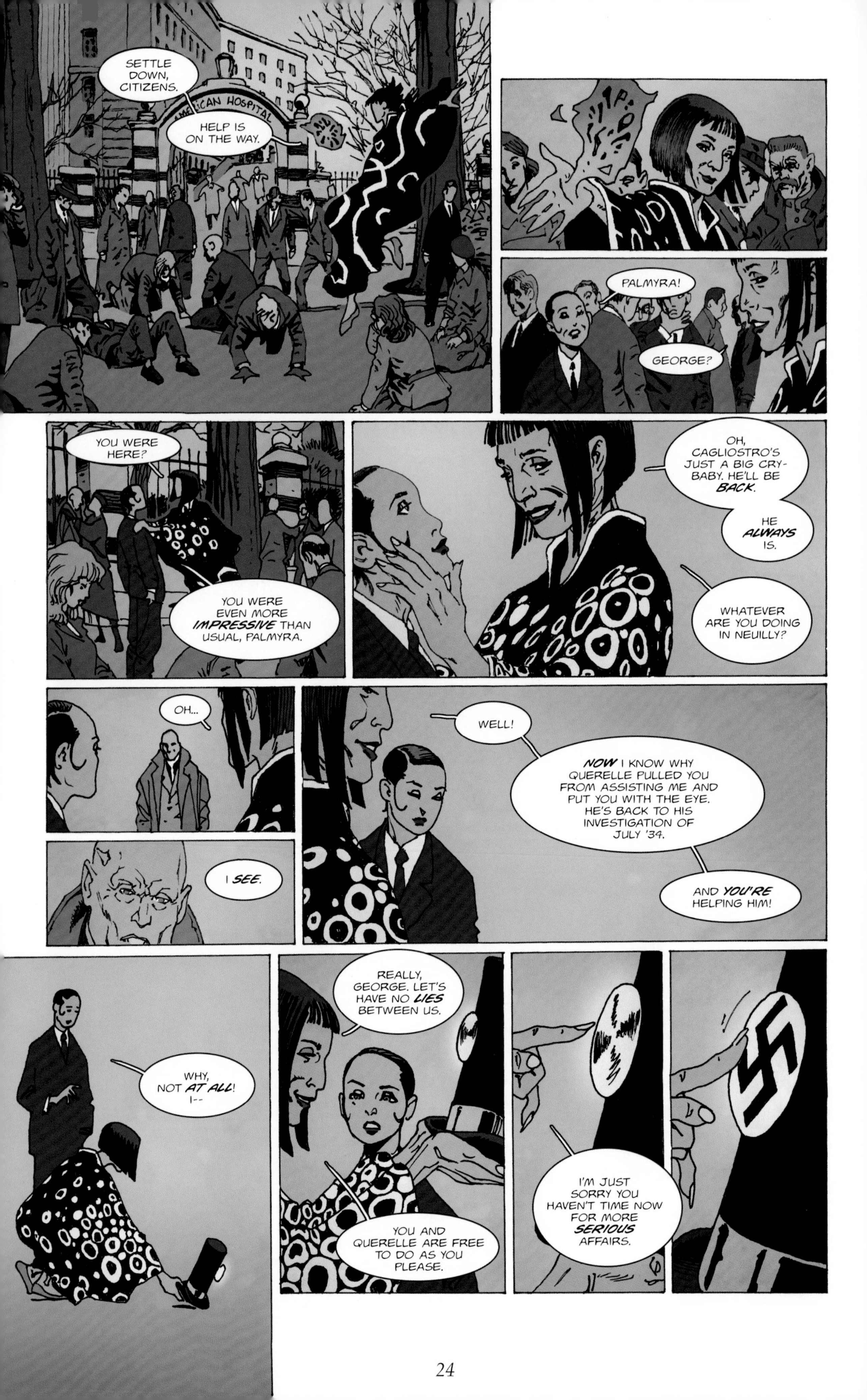
SETTLE DOWN, CITIZENS.
HELP IS ON THE WAY.
AMERICAN HOSPITAL
PALMYRA!
GEORGE?
YOU WERE HERE?
YOU WERE EVEN MORE *IMPRESSIVE* THAN USUAL, PALMYRA.
OH, CAGLIOSTRO'S JUST A BIG CRY-BABY. HE'LL BE *BACK*.
HE *ALWAYS* IS.
WHATEVER ARE YOU DOING IN NEUILLY?
OH...
I *SEE*.
WELL!
NOW I KNOW WHY QUERELLE PULLED YOU FROM ASSISTING ME AND PUT YOU WITH THE EYE. HE'S BACK TO HIS INVESTIGATION OF JULY '34.
AND *YOU'RE* HELPING HIM!
WHY, NOT *AT ALL*! I--
REALLY, GEORGE. LET'S HAVE NO *LIES* BETWEEN US.
YOU AND QUERELLE ARE FREE TO DO AS YOU PLEASE.
I'M JUST SORRY YOU HAVEN'T TIME NOW FOR MORE *SERIOUS* AFFAIRS.

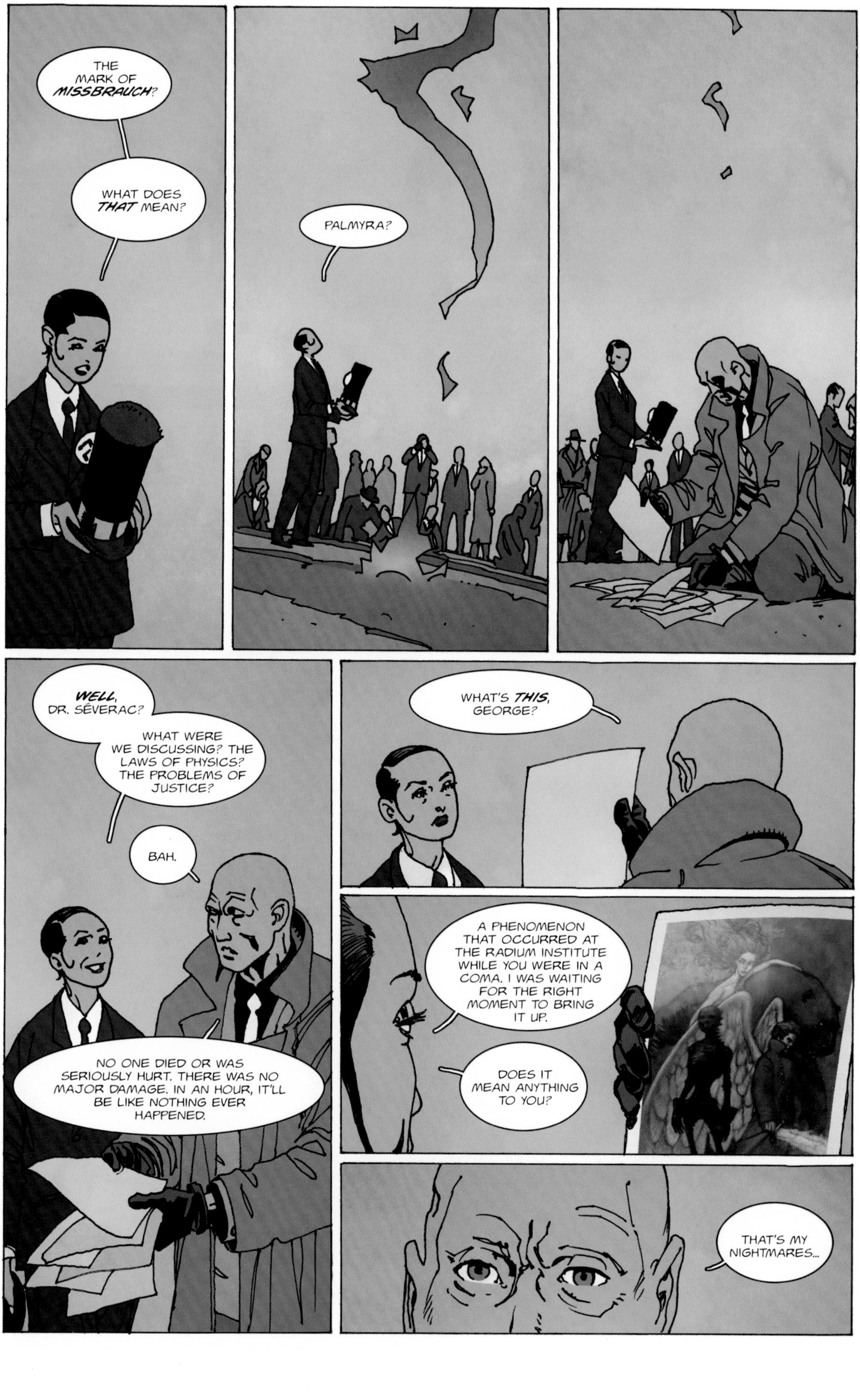
THE MARK OF *MISSBRAUCH*?
WHAT DOES *THAT* MEAN?
PALMYRA?
WELL, DR. SÉVERAC?
WHAT WERE WE DISCUSSING? THE LAWS OF PHYSICS? THE PROBLEMS OF JUSTICE?
BAH.
NO ONE DIED OR WAS SERIOUSLY HURT. THERE WAS NO MAJOR DAMAGE. IN AN HOUR, IT'LL BE LIKE NOTHING EVER HAPPENED.
WHAT'S *THIS*, GEORGE?
A PHENOMENON THAT OCCURRED AT THE RADIUM INSTITUTE WHILE YOU WERE IN A COMA. I WAS WAITING FOR THE RIGHT MOMENT TO BRING IT UP.
DOES IT MEAN ANYTHING TO YOU?
THAT'S MY NIGHTMARES...

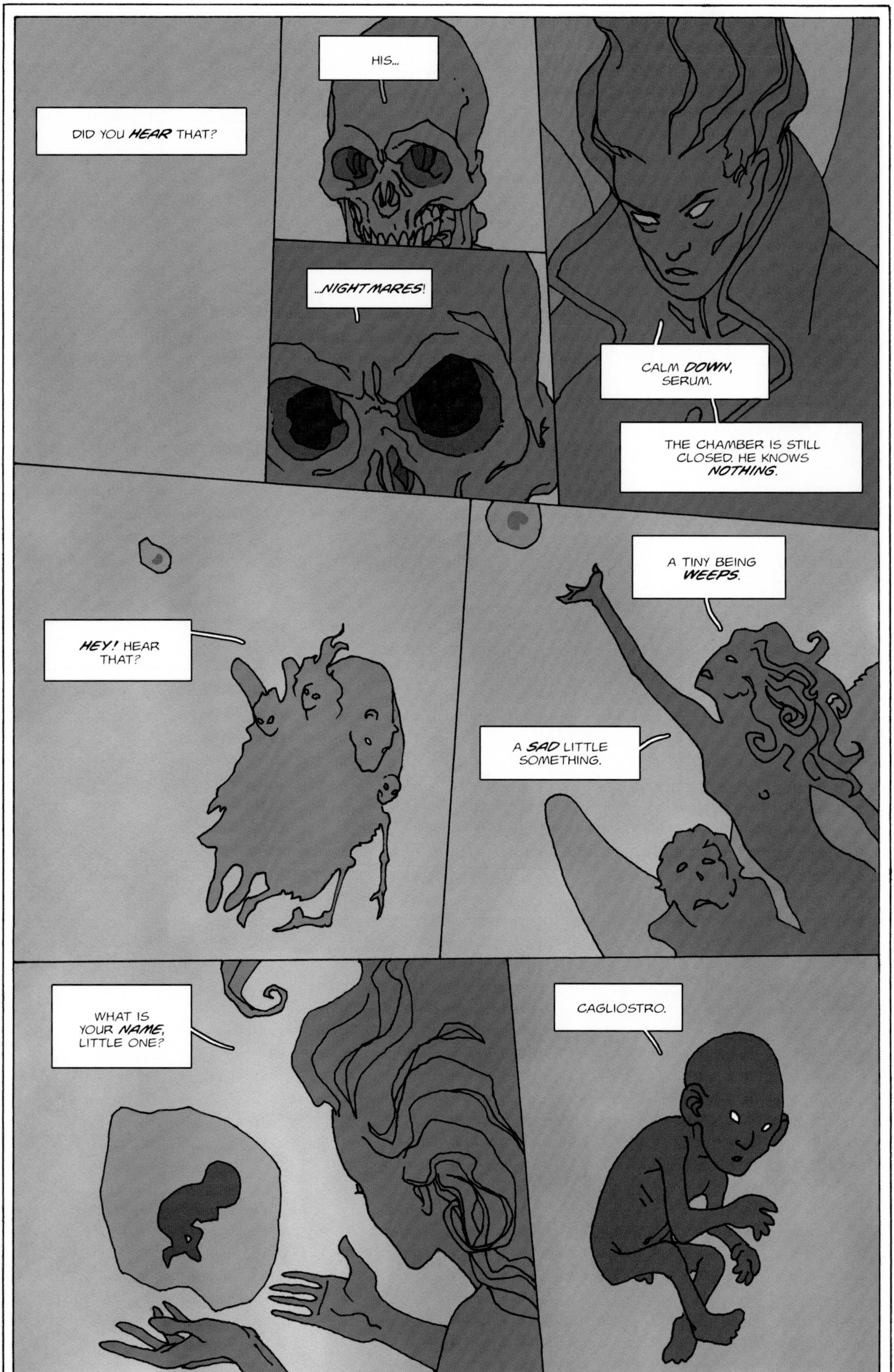
DID YOU HEAR THAT?
HIS...
...NIGHTMARES!
CALM DOWN, SERUM.
THE CHAMBER IS STILL CLOSED. HE KNOWS NOTHING.
HEY! HEAR THAT?
A TINY BEING WEEPS.
A SAD LITTLE SOMETHING.
WHAT IS YOUR NAME, LITTLE ONE?
CAGLIOSTRO.

THE BURNING CHAMBER

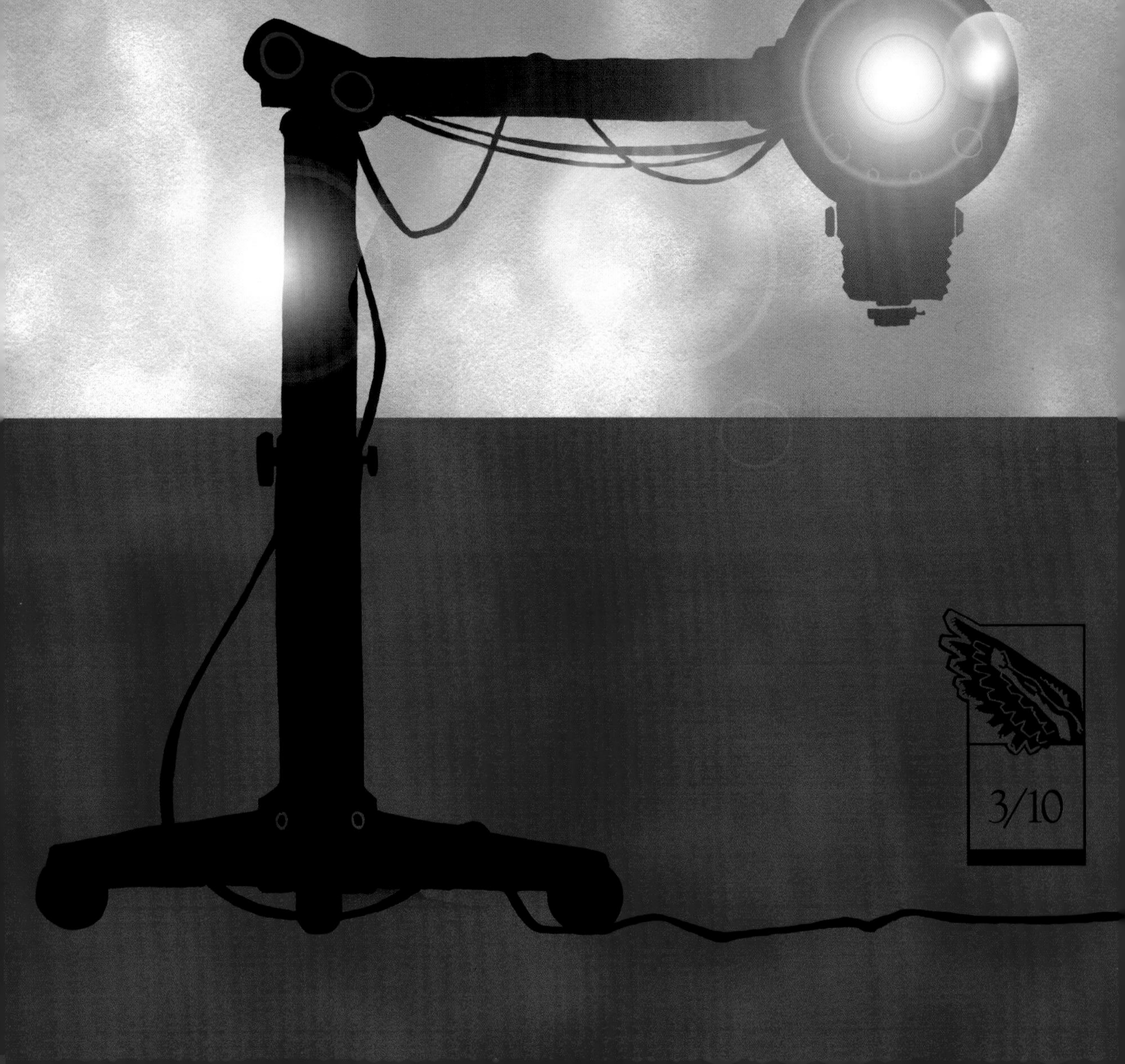
3/10

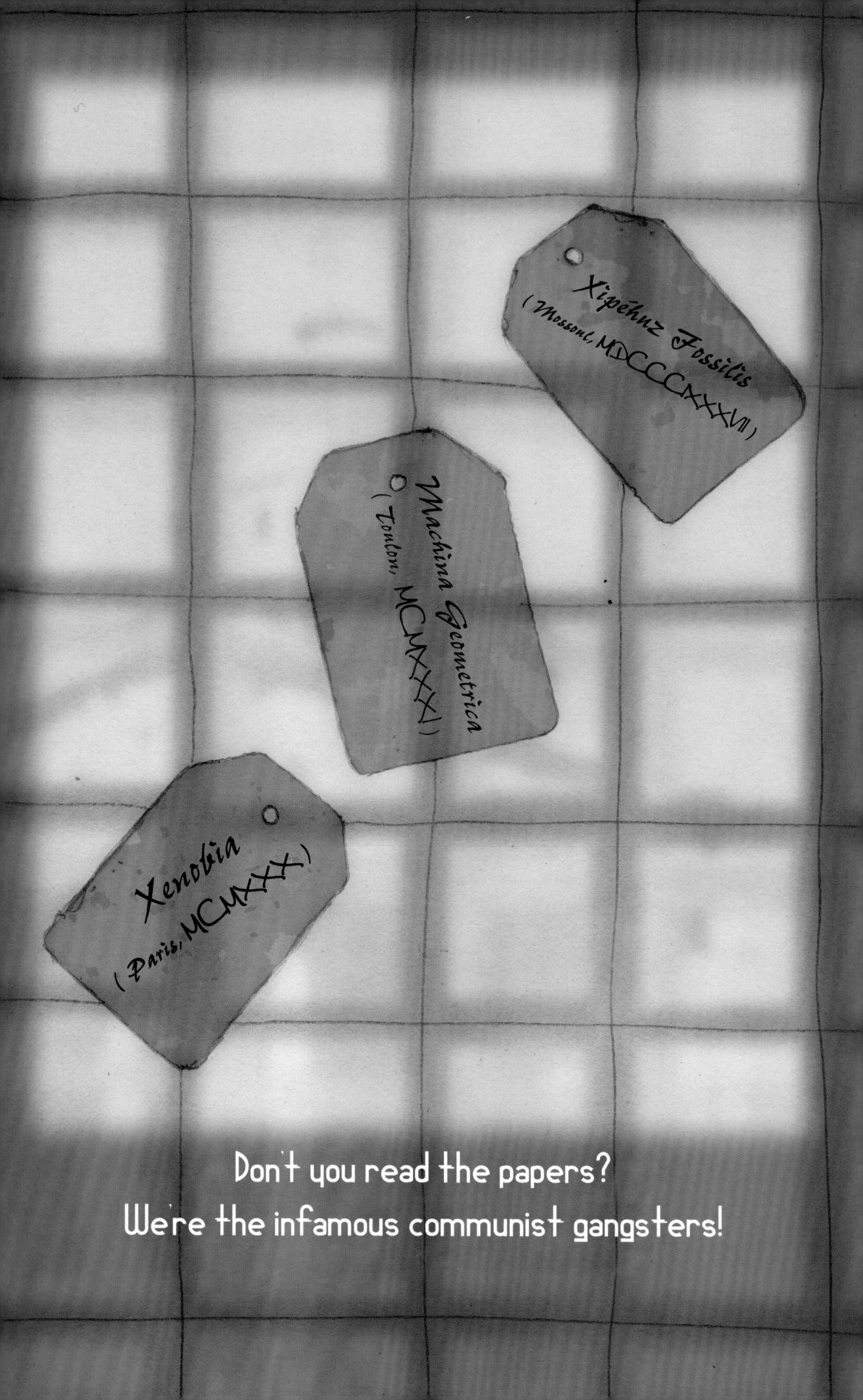
Xipéhuz Fossilis
(Mossoul, MDCCCXXXVII)
Machina Geometrica
(Tonton, MCMXXXI)
Xenobia
(Paris, MCMXXX)
Don't you read the papers?
We're the infamous communist gangsters!

URANIUM 235.

HEAVY WATER.

GOOD GOD! IT COULD WORK!

CRITICAL MASS.

FRÉDÉRIC?

YES, MY DEAR?

THE RADIUM INSTITUTE. 1:50 PM.

I STARTED DOING THE INVENTORY OF THE STORES AGAIN. LOOK WHAT I FOUND.

A XIPEHUZ!

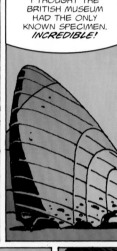

I THOUGHT THE BRITISH MUSEUM HAD THE ONLY KNOWN SPECIMEN. INCREDIBLE!

DO YOU REMEMBER THIS? THE INVASION OF PARIS TEN YEARS AGO.

MOTHER MUST HAVE BEEN MAD TO KEEP IT HERE!

ON THE OTHER HAND, THIS FRAGMENT OF A DIMENSIONAL MACHINE IS WORTH ITS WEIGHT IN GOLD.

WE COULD SELL IT TO THE AMERICANS IF--

DING!

HUH? AT THIS HOUR?

HOW'S YOUR RESEARCH GOING?

MOVING ALONG.

ACTUALLY, IT'S GOING SO WELL IT'S TERRIFYING.

IS AN OLD SOLDIER STILL WELCOME HERE?

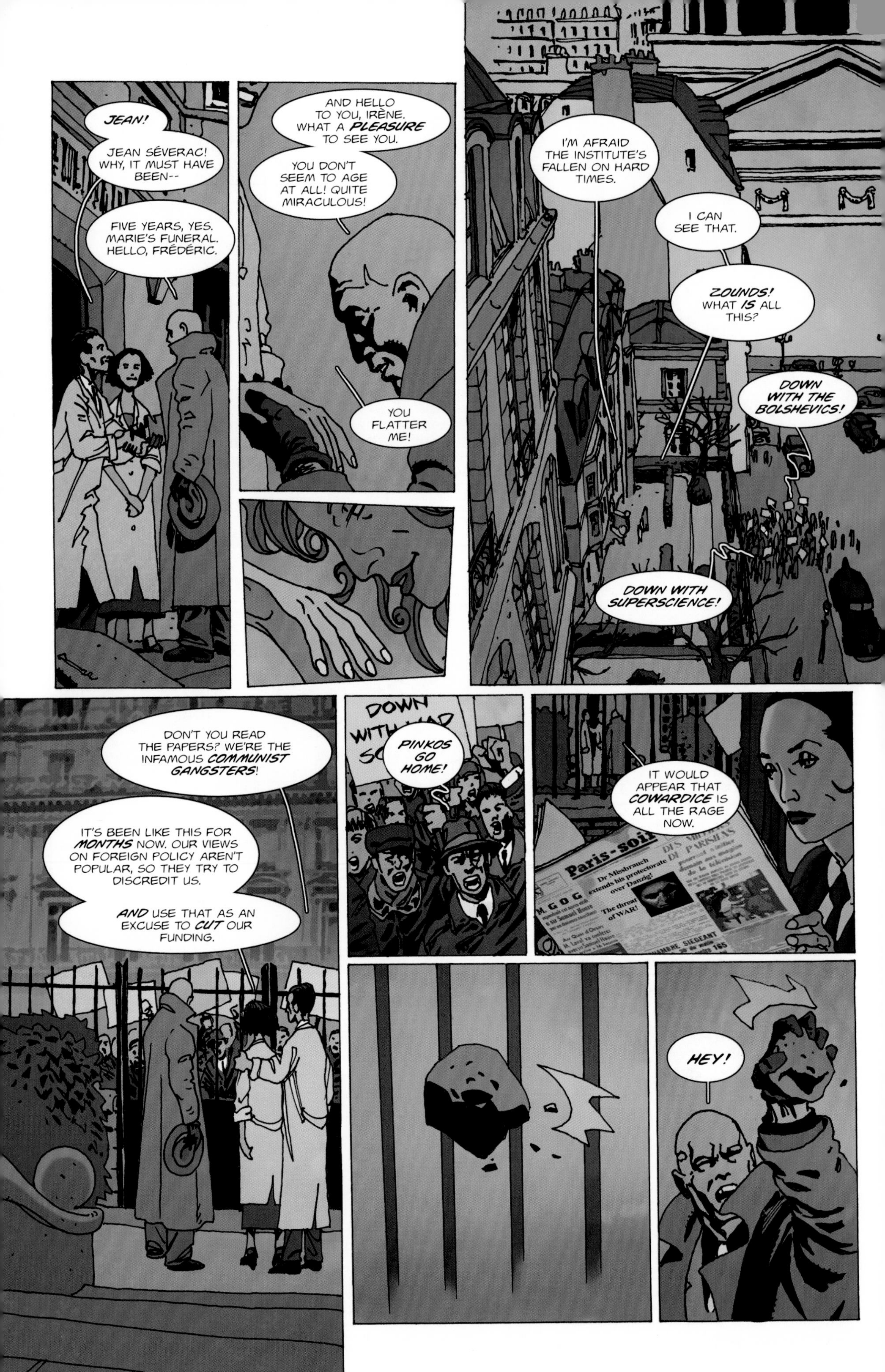

JEAN!
JEAN SÉVERAC! WHY, IT MUST HAVE BEEN--
FIVE YEARS, YES. MARIE'S FUNERAL. HELLO, FRÉDÉRIC.
AND HELLO TO YOU, IRÈNE. WHAT A PLEASURE TO SEE YOU.
YOU DON'T SEEM TO AGE AT ALL! QUITE MIRACULOUS!
YOU FLATTER ME!
I'M AFRAID THE INSTITUTE'S FALLEN ON HARD TIMES.
I CAN SEE THAT.
ZOUNDS! WHAT IS ALL THIS?
DOWN WITH THE BOLSHEVICS!
DOWN WITH SUPERSCIENCE!
DON'T YOU READ THE PAPERS? WE'RE THE INFAMOUS COMMUNIST GANGSTERS!
IT'S BEEN LIKE THIS FOR MONTHS NOW. OUR VIEWS ON FOREIGN POLICY AREN'T POPULAR, SO THEY TRY TO DISCREDIT US.
AND USE THAT AS AN EXCUSE TO CUT OUR FUNDING.
PINKOS GO HOME!
IT WOULD APPEAR THAT COWARDICE IS ALL THE RAGE NOW.
Paris-soir
Dr Missbrauch extends his protectorate over Danzig!
The threat of WAR!
HEY!

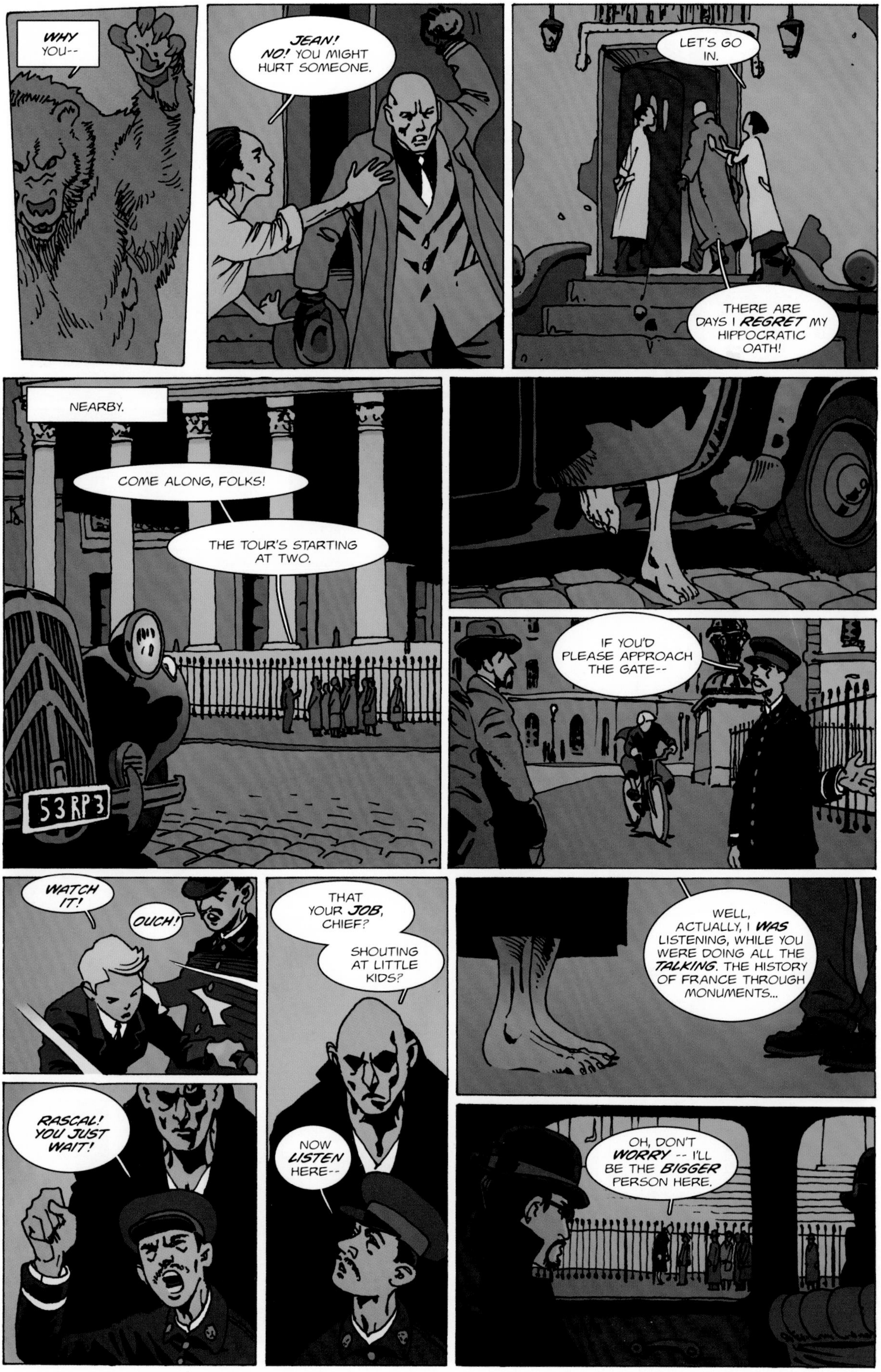

WHY YOU--
JEAN! NO! YOU MIGHT HURT SOMEONE.
LET'S GO IN.
THERE ARE DAYS I REGRET MY HIPPOCRATIC OATH!
NEARBY.
COME ALONG, FOLKS!
THE TOUR'S STARTING AT TWO.
IF YOU'D PLEASE APPROACH THE GATE--
WATCH IT!
OUCH!
RASCAL! YOU JUST WAIT!
THAT YOUR JOB, CHIEF?
SHOUTING AT LITTLE KIDS?
NOW LISTEN HERE--
WELL, ACTUALLY, I WAS LISTENING, WHILE YOU WERE DOING ALL THE TALKING. THE HISTORY OF FRANCE THROUGH MONUMENTS...
OH, DON'T WORRY -- I'LL BE THE BIGGER PERSON HERE.

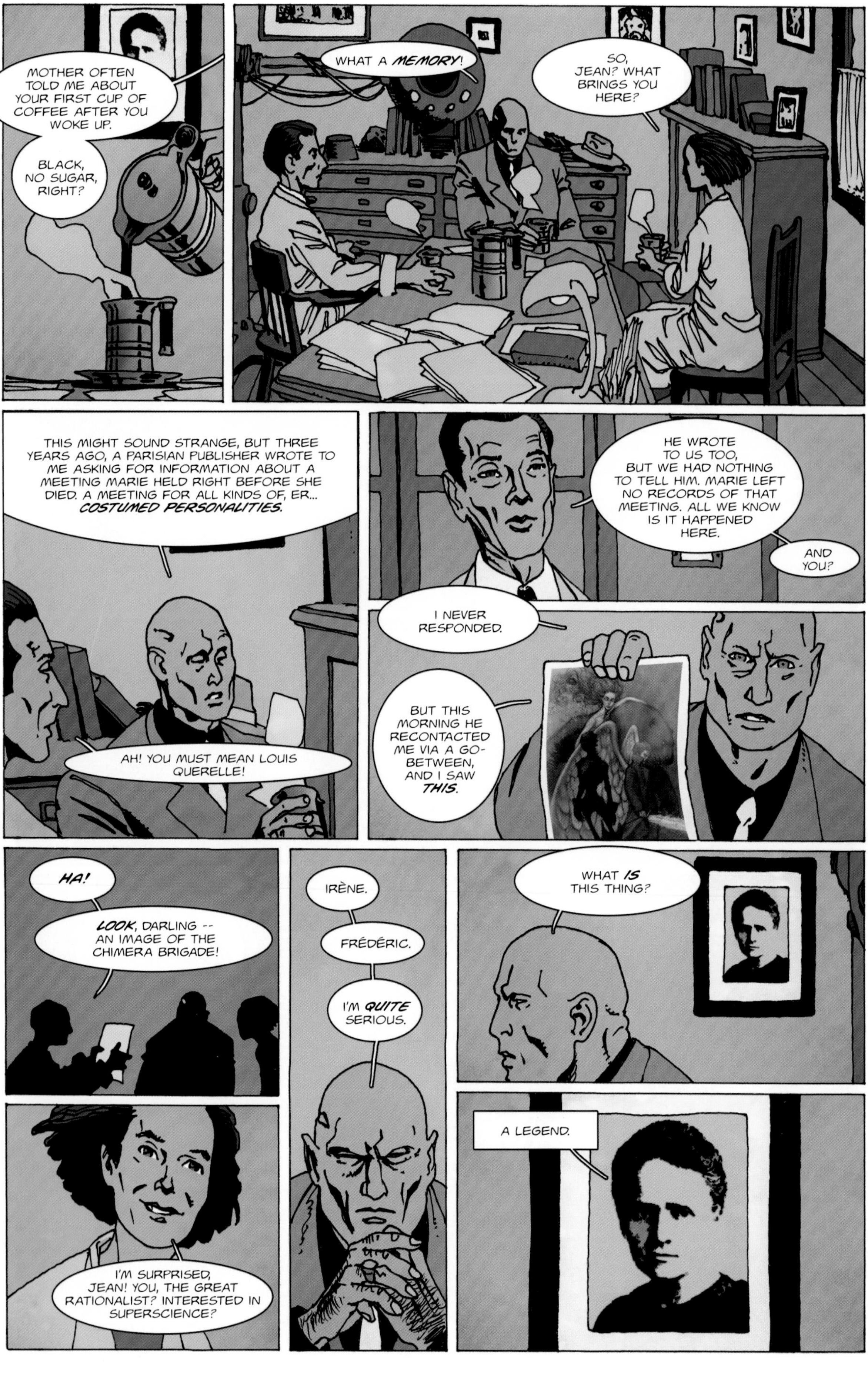
MOTHER OFTEN TOLD ME ABOUT YOUR FIRST CUP OF COFFEE AFTER YOU WOKE UP.
BLACK, NO SUGAR, RIGHT?
WHAT A MEMORY!
SO, JEAN? WHAT BRINGS YOU HERE?
THIS MIGHT SOUND STRANGE, BUT THREE YEARS AGO, A PARISIAN PUBLISHER WROTE TO ME ASKING FOR INFORMATION ABOUT A MEETING MARIE HELD RIGHT BEFORE SHE DIED. A MEETING FOR ALL KINDS OF, ER... COSTUMED PERSONALITIES.
AH! YOU MUST MEAN LOUIS QUERELLE!
HE WROTE TO US TOO, BUT WE HAD NOTHING TO TELL HIM. MARIE LEFT NO RECORDS OF THAT MEETING. ALL WE KNOW IS IT HAPPENED HERE.
AND YOU?
I NEVER RESPONDED.
BUT THIS MORNING HE RECONTACTED ME VIA A GO-BETWEEN, AND I SAW THIS.
HA!
LOOK, DARLING -- AN IMAGE OF THE CHIMERA BRIGADE!
I'M SURPRISED, JEAN! YOU, THE GREAT RATIONALIST? INTERESTED IN SUPERSCIENCE?
IRÈNE.
FRÉDÉRIC.
I'M QUITE SERIOUS.
WHAT IS THIS THING?
A LEGEND.

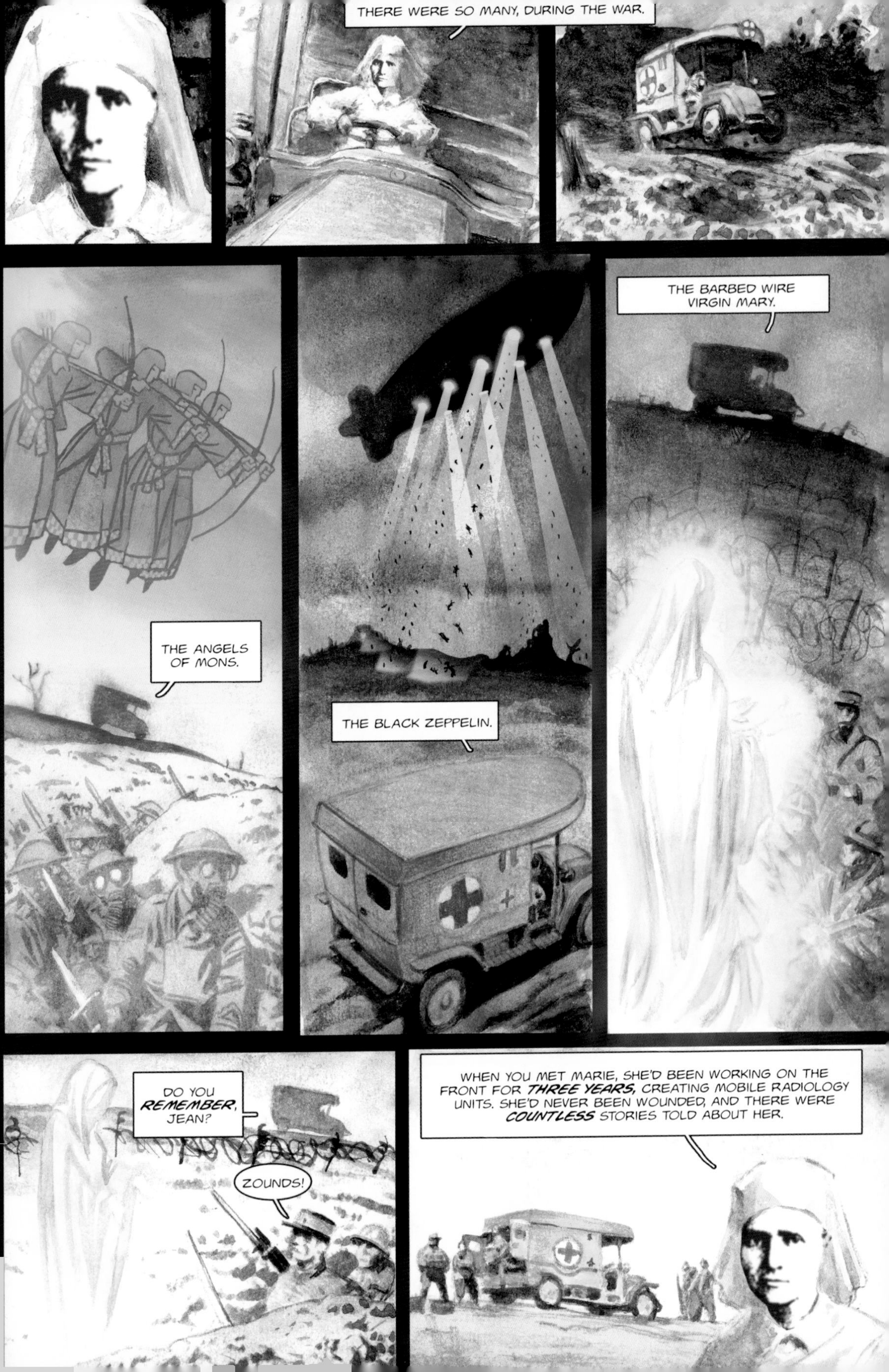
THERE WERE SO MANY, DURING THE WAR.
THE ANGELS OF MONS.
THE BLACK ZEPPELIN.
THE BARBED WIRE VIRGIN MARY.
DO YOU REMEMBER, JEAN?
ZOUNDS!
WHEN YOU MET MARIE, SHE'D BEEN WORKING ON THE FRONT FOR THREE YEARS, CREATING MOBILE RADIOLOGY UNITS. SHE'D NEVER BEEN WOUNDED, AND THERE WERE COUNTLESS STORIES TOLD ABOUT HER.

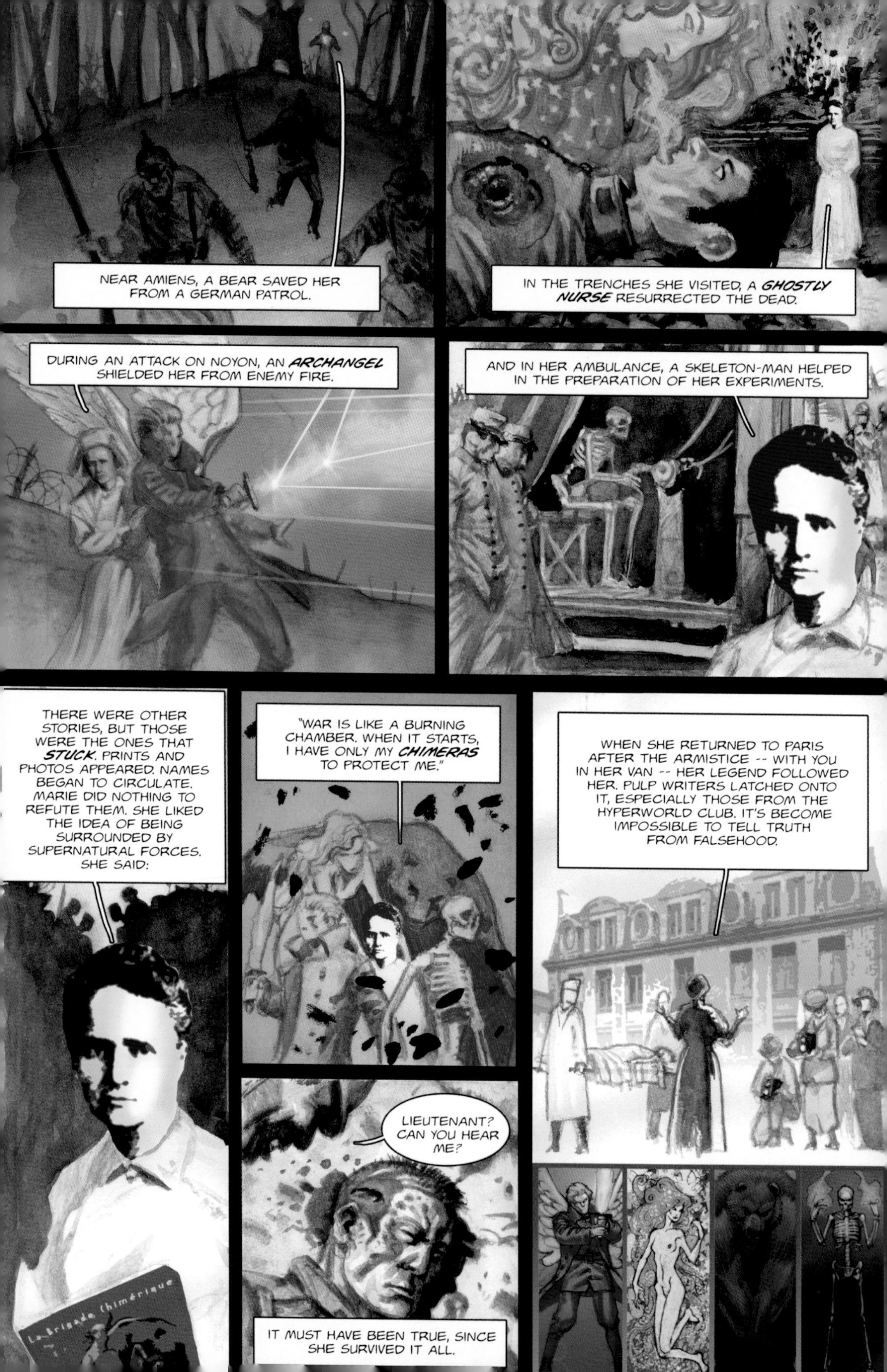

NEAR AMIENS, A BEAR SAVED HER FROM A GERMAN PATROL.
IN THE TRENCHES SHE VISITED, A GHOSTLY NURSE RESURRECTED THE DEAD.
DURING AN ATTACK ON NOYON, AN ARCHANGEL SHIELDED HER FROM ENEMY FIRE.
AND IN HER AMBULANCE, A SKELETON-MAN HELPED IN THE PREPARATION OF HER EXPERIMENTS.
THERE WERE OTHER STORIES, BUT THOSE WERE THE ONES THAT STUCK. PRINTS AND PHOTOS APPEARED. NAMES BEGAN TO CIRCULATE. MARIE DID NOTHING TO REFUTE THEM. SHE LIKED THE IDEA OF BEING SURROUNDED BY SUPERNATURAL FORCES. SHE SAID:
"WAR IS LIKE A BURNING CHAMBER. WHEN IT STARTS, I HAVE ONLY MY CHIMERAS TO PROTECT ME."
La Brigade Chimérique
LIEUTENANT? CAN YOU HEAR ME?
IT MUST HAVE BEEN TRUE, SINCE SHE SURVIVED IT ALL.
WHEN SHE RETURNED TO PARIS AFTER THE ARMISTICE -- WITH YOU IN HER VAN -- HER LEGEND FOLLOWED HER. PULP WRITERS LATCHED ONTO IT, ESPECIALLY THOSE FROM THE HYPERWORLD CLUB. IT'S BECOME IMPOSSIBLE TO TELL TRUTH FROM FALSEHOOD.

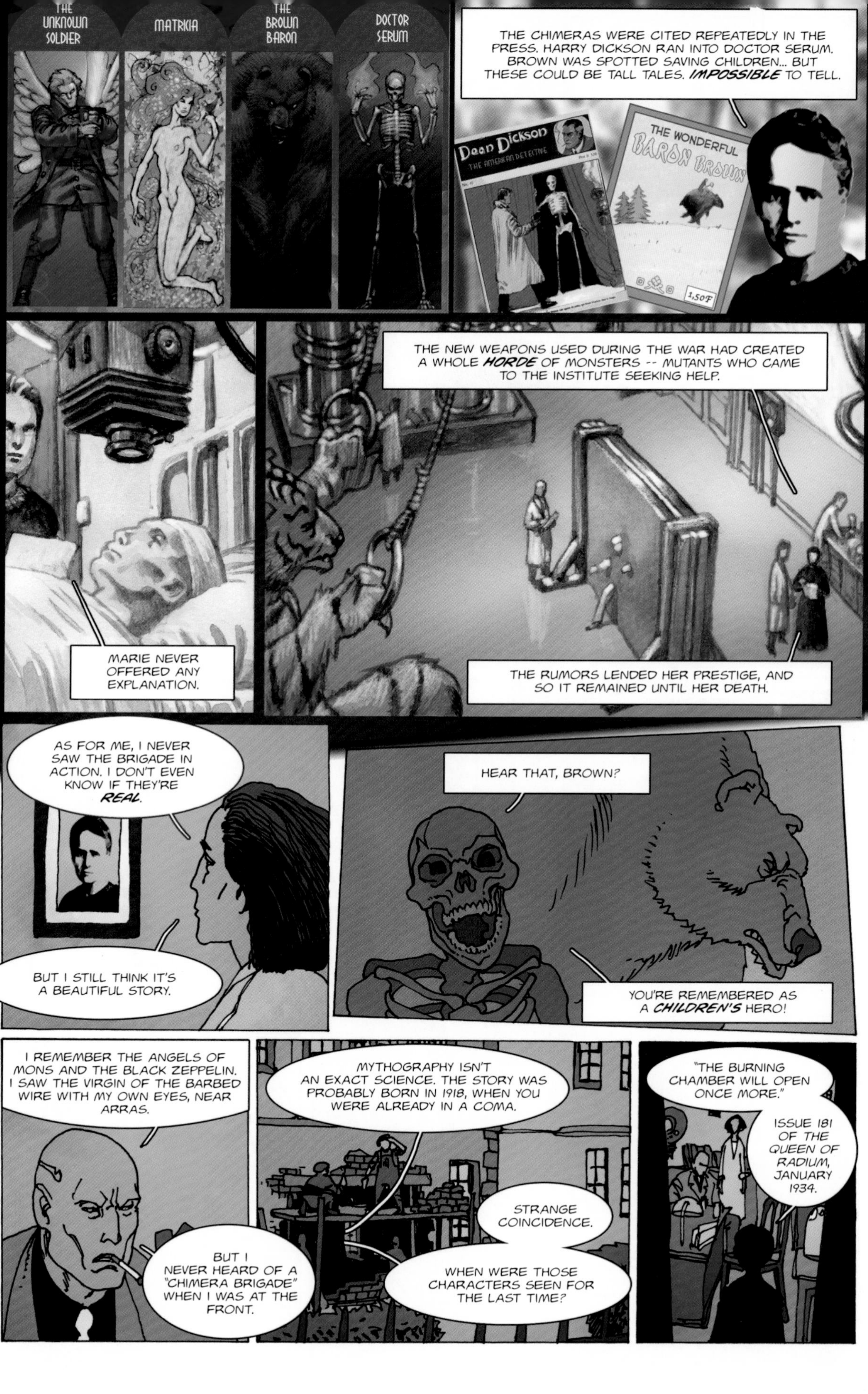
THE UNKNOWN SOLDIER
MATRKIA
THE BROWN BARON
DOCTOR SERUM
THE CHIMERAS WERE CITED REPEATEDLY IN THE PRESS. HARRY DICKSON RAN INTO DOCTOR SERUM. BROWN WAS SPOTTED SAVING CHILDREN... BUT THESE COULD BE TALL TALES. *IMPOSSIBLE* TO TELL.
Dean Dickson
THE AMERICAN DETECTIVE
THE WONDERFUL
BARON BROWN
1,50F
MARIE NEVER OFFERED ANY EXPLANATION.
THE NEW WEAPONS USED DURING THE WAR HAD CREATED A WHOLE *HORDE* OF MONSTERS -- MUTANTS WHO CAME TO THE INSTITUTE SEEKING HELP.
THE RUMORS LENDED HER PRESTIGE, AND SO IT REMAINED UNTIL HER DEATH.
AS FOR ME, I NEVER SAW THE BRIGADE IN ACTION. I DON'T EVEN KNOW IF THEY'RE *REAL*.
BUT I STILL THINK IT'S A BEAUTIFUL STORY.
HEAR THAT, BROWN?
YOU'RE REMEMBERED AS A *CHILDREN'S* HERO!
I REMEMBER THE ANGELS OF MONS AND THE BLACK ZEPPELIN. I SAW THE VIRGIN OF THE BARBED WIRE WITH MY OWN EYES, NEAR ARRAS.
BUT I NEVER HEARD OF A "CHIMERA BRIGADE" WHEN I WAS AT THE FRONT.
MYTHOGRAPHY ISN'T AN EXACT SCIENCE. THE STORY WAS PROBABLY BORN IN 1918, WHEN YOU WERE ALREADY IN A COMA.
STRANGE COINCIDENCE.
WHEN WERE THOSE CHARACTERS SEEN FOR THE LAST TIME?
"THE BURNING CHAMBER WILL OPEN ONCE MORE."
ISSUE 181 OF THE QUEEN OF RADIUM, JANUARY 1934.

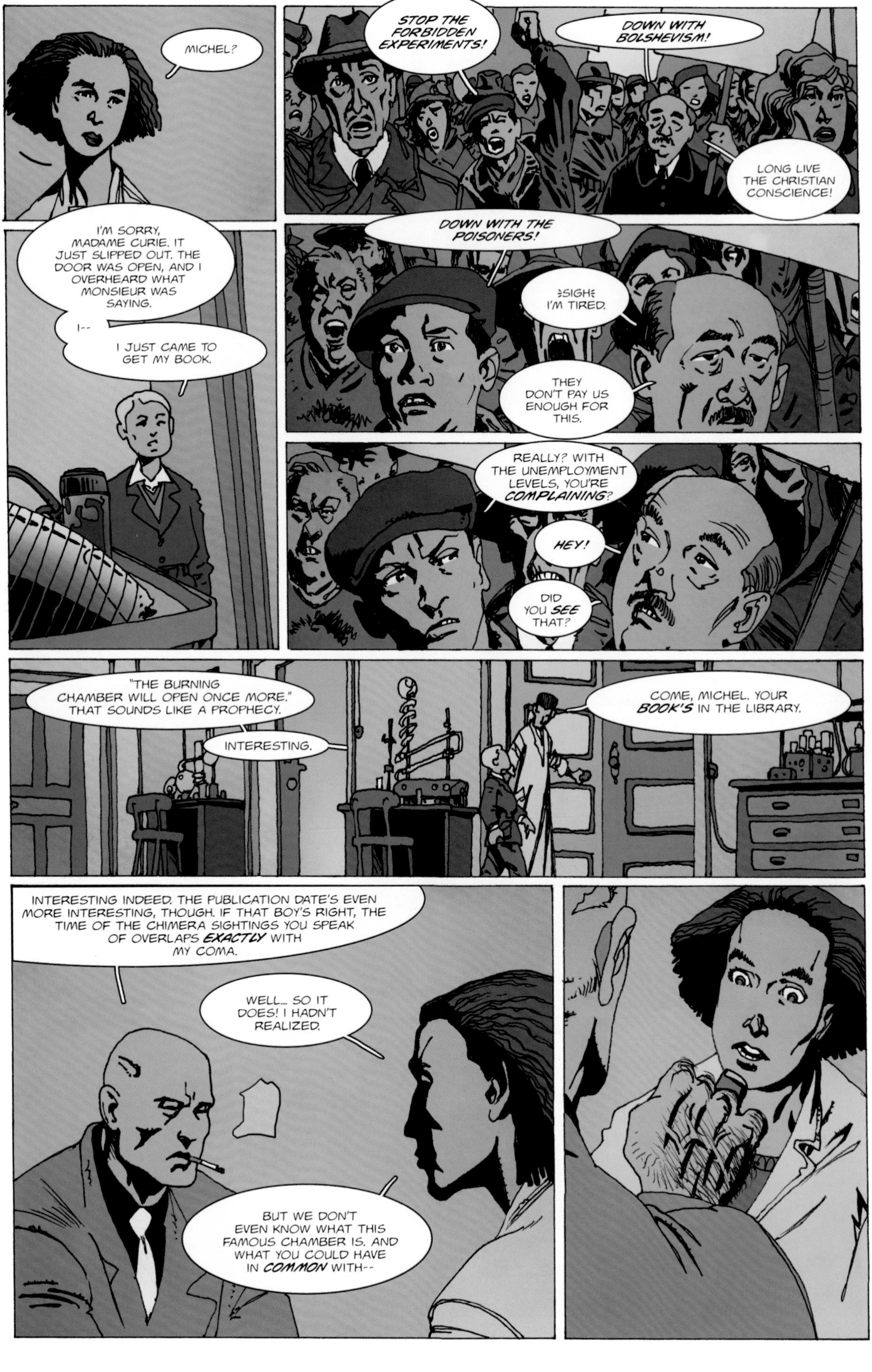
MICHEL?
STOP THE FORBIDDEN EXPERIMENTS!
DOWN WITH BOLSHEVISM!
LONG LIVE THE CHRISTIAN CONSCIENCE!
I'M SORRY, MADAME CURIE. IT JUST SLIPPED OUT. THE DOOR WAS OPEN, AND I OVERHEARD WHAT MONSIEUR WAS SAYING.
I--
I JUST CAME TO GET MY BOOK.
DOWN WITH THE POISONERS!
≑SIGH≑ I'M TIRED.
THEY DON'T PAY US ENOUGH FOR THIS.
REALLY? WITH THE UNEMPLOYMENT LEVELS, YOU'RE COMPLAINING?
HEY!
DID YOU SEE THAT?
"THE BURNING CHAMBER WILL OPEN ONCE MORE." THAT SOUNDS LIKE A PROPHECY.
INTERESTING.
COME, MICHEL. YOUR BOOK'S IN THE LIBRARY.
INTERESTING INDEED. THE PUBLICATION DATE'S EVEN MORE INTERESTING, THOUGH. IF THAT BOY'S RIGHT, THE TIME OF THE CHIMERA SIGHTINGS YOU SPEAK OF OVERLAPS EXACTLY WITH MY COMA.
WELL... SO IT DOES! I HADN'T REALIZED.
BUT WE DON'T EVEN KNOW WHAT THIS FAMOUS CHAMBER IS. AND WHAT YOU COULD HAVE IN COMMON WITH--

JEAN!

WHAT *IS* THAT?

WHAT DOES THAT RING *MEAN*?

THAT'S THE SÉVERAC COAT-OF-ARMS.

IT DATES FROM THE 13TH CENTURY. THE 4TH CRUSADE, TO BE EXACT. I KNOW IT WELL—I GREW UP WITH IT AND I'VE DREAMED OF IT EVERY NIGHT SINCE I WOKE UP.

SO LET *ME* ASK *YOU*, IRÈNE...

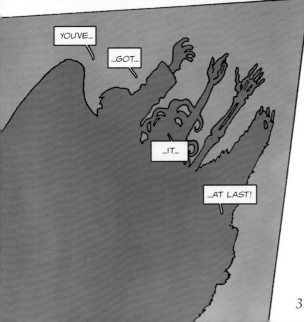

YOU'VE...

...GOT...

...IT...

...AT LAST!

WHAT EXACTLY DID MARIE *DO* TO ME DURING MY SIXTEEN YEARS HERE?

PROFESSOR CURIE? *PROFESSOR*!

COME RIGHT AWAY! THERE'S SOMETHING *TERRIBLE* GOING ON OUTSIDE!

WHA--

WATCH OUT!

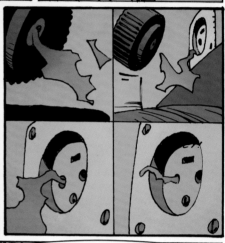

JEAN! DID YOU *SEE* THAT? DID SOMETHING GET OUT OF THE BOTTLE?

I DON'T *THINK* SO--

FRÉDÉRIC JOLIOT! IRÈNE CURIE!

COME AND SEE WHAT YOU BASTARDS HAVE DONE TO ME!

SWINDLERS! BUTCHERS! SCIENTIFIC FILTH!

IT'S COMING FROM THE COURTYARD.

THEY WILL *PRAISE MY NAME* FOR CRUSHING YOU!

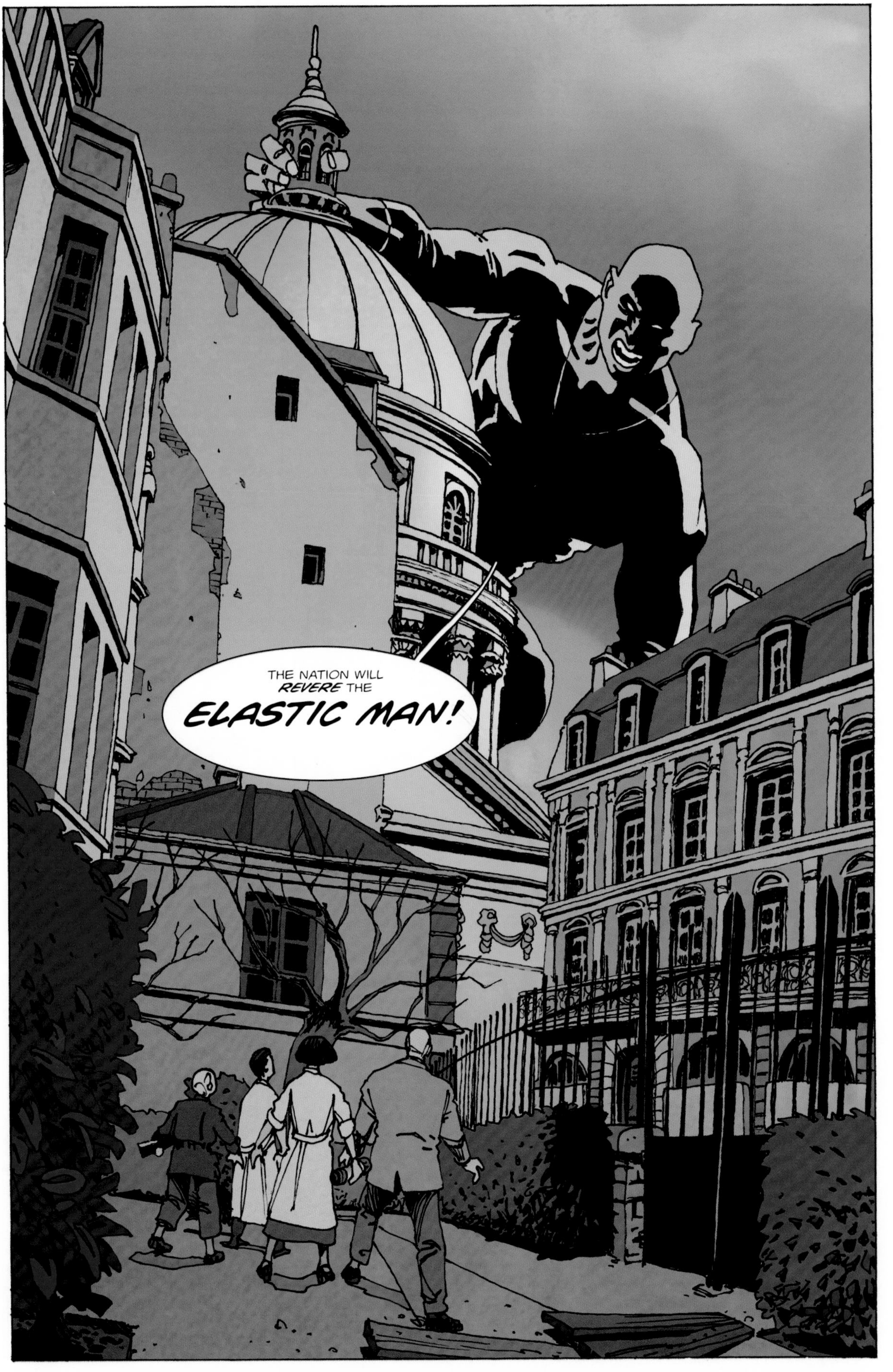
THE NATION WILL *REVERE* THE
ELASTIC MAN!

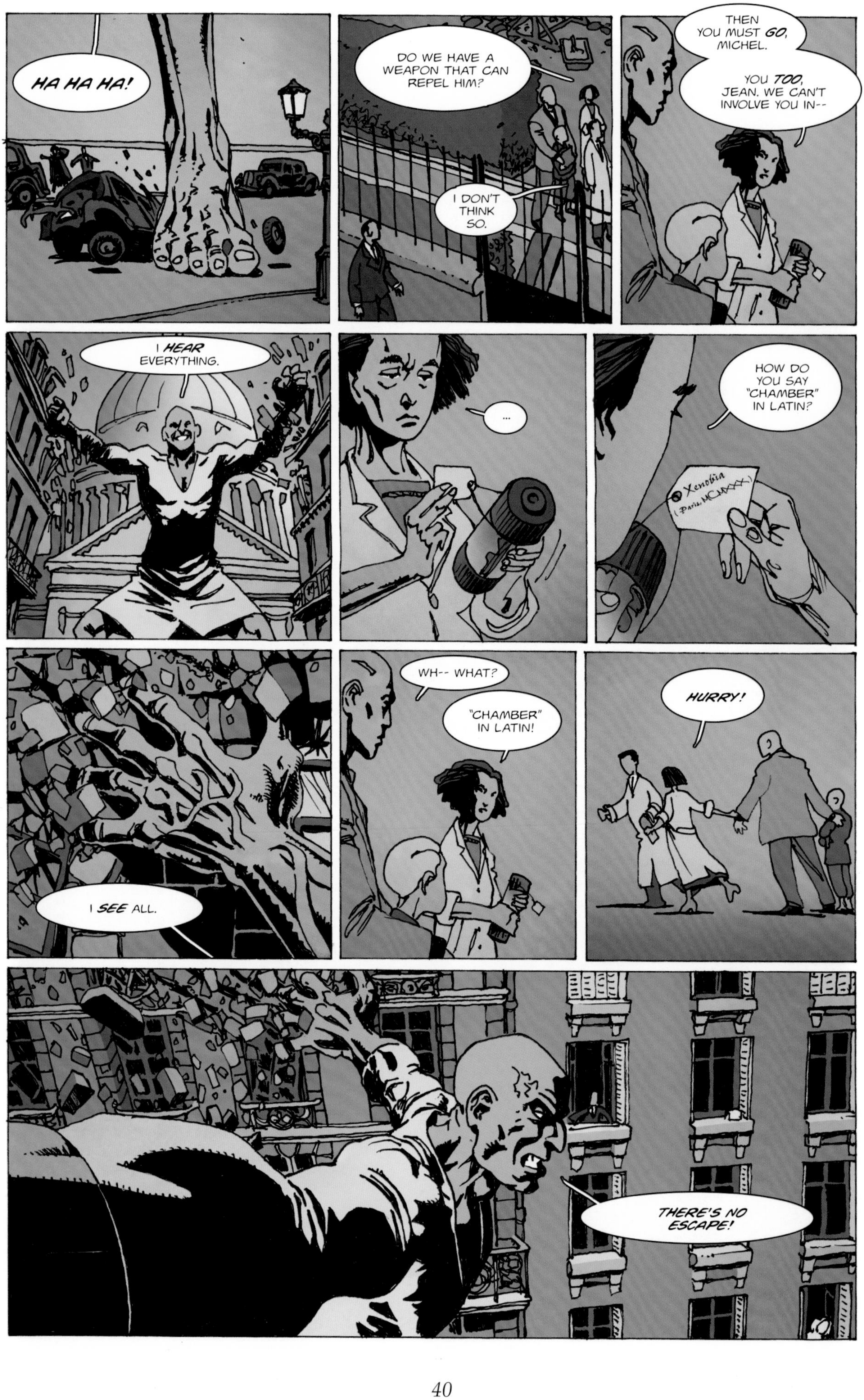
HA HA HA!
DO WE HAVE A WEAPON THAT CAN REPEL HIM?
I DON'T THINK SO.
THEN YOU MUST GO, MICHEL.
YOU TOO, JEAN. WE CAN'T INVOLVE YOU IN--
I HEAR EVERYTHING.
...
HOW DO YOU SAY "CHAMBER" IN LATIN?
Xenobia
I SEE ALL.
WH-- WHAT?
"CHAMBER" IN LATIN!
HURRY!
THERE'S NO ESCAPE!

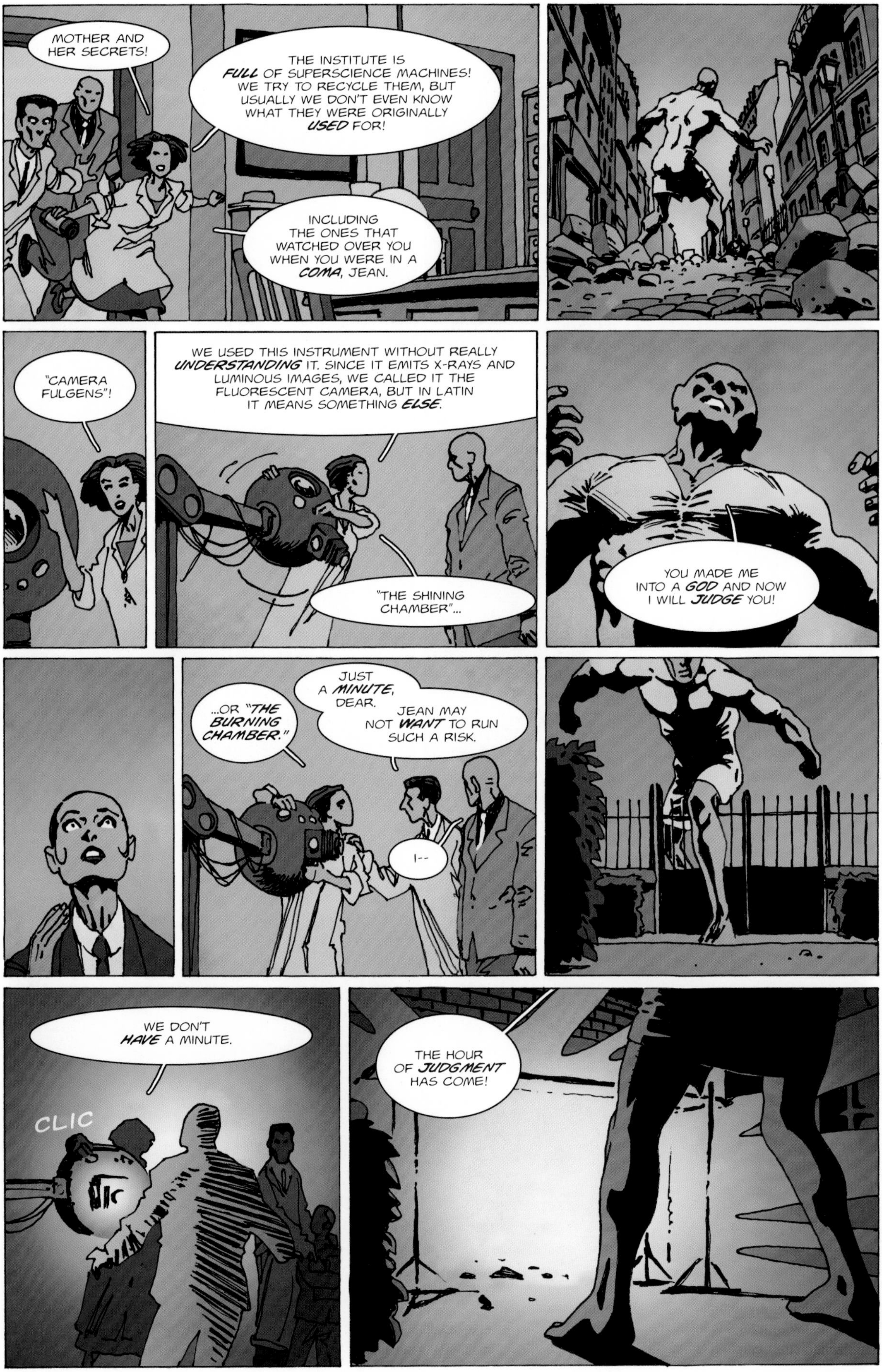
MOTHER AND HER SECRETS!
THE INSTITUTE IS FULL OF SUPERSCIENCE MACHINES! WE TRY TO RECYCLE THEM, BUT USUALLY WE DON'T EVEN KNOW WHAT THEY WERE ORIGINALLY USED FOR!
INCLUDING THE ONES THAT WATCHED OVER YOU WHEN YOU WERE IN A COMA, JEAN.
"CAMERA FULGENS"!
WE USED THIS INSTRUMENT WITHOUT REALLY UNDERSTANDING IT. SINCE IT EMITS X-RAYS AND LUMINOUS IMAGES, WE CALLED IT THE FLUORESCENT CAMERA, BUT IN LATIN IT MEANS SOMETHING ELSE.
"THE SHINING CHAMBER"...
YOU MADE ME INTO A GOD AND NOW I WILL JUDGE YOU!
...OR "THE BURNING CHAMBER."
JUST A MINUTE, DEAR.
JEAN MAY NOT WANT TO RUN SUCH A RISK.
I--
WE DON'T HAVE A MINUTE.
CLIC
THE HOUR OF JUDGMENT HAS COME!

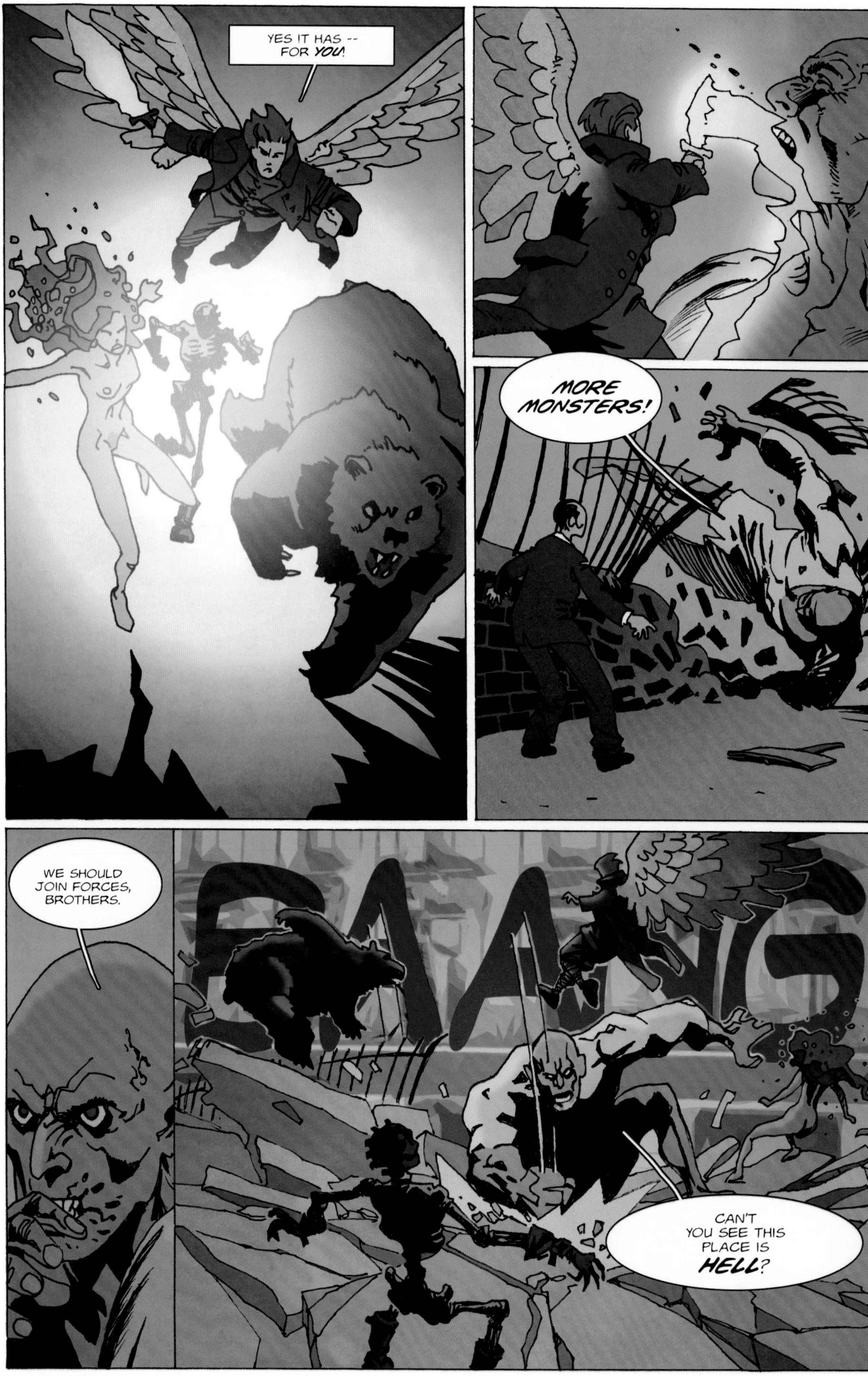
YES IT HAS -- FOR *YOU*!
MORE MONSTERS!
WE SHOULD JOIN FORCES, BROTHERS.
BAAANG
CAN'T YOU SEE THIS PLACE IS ***HELL***?

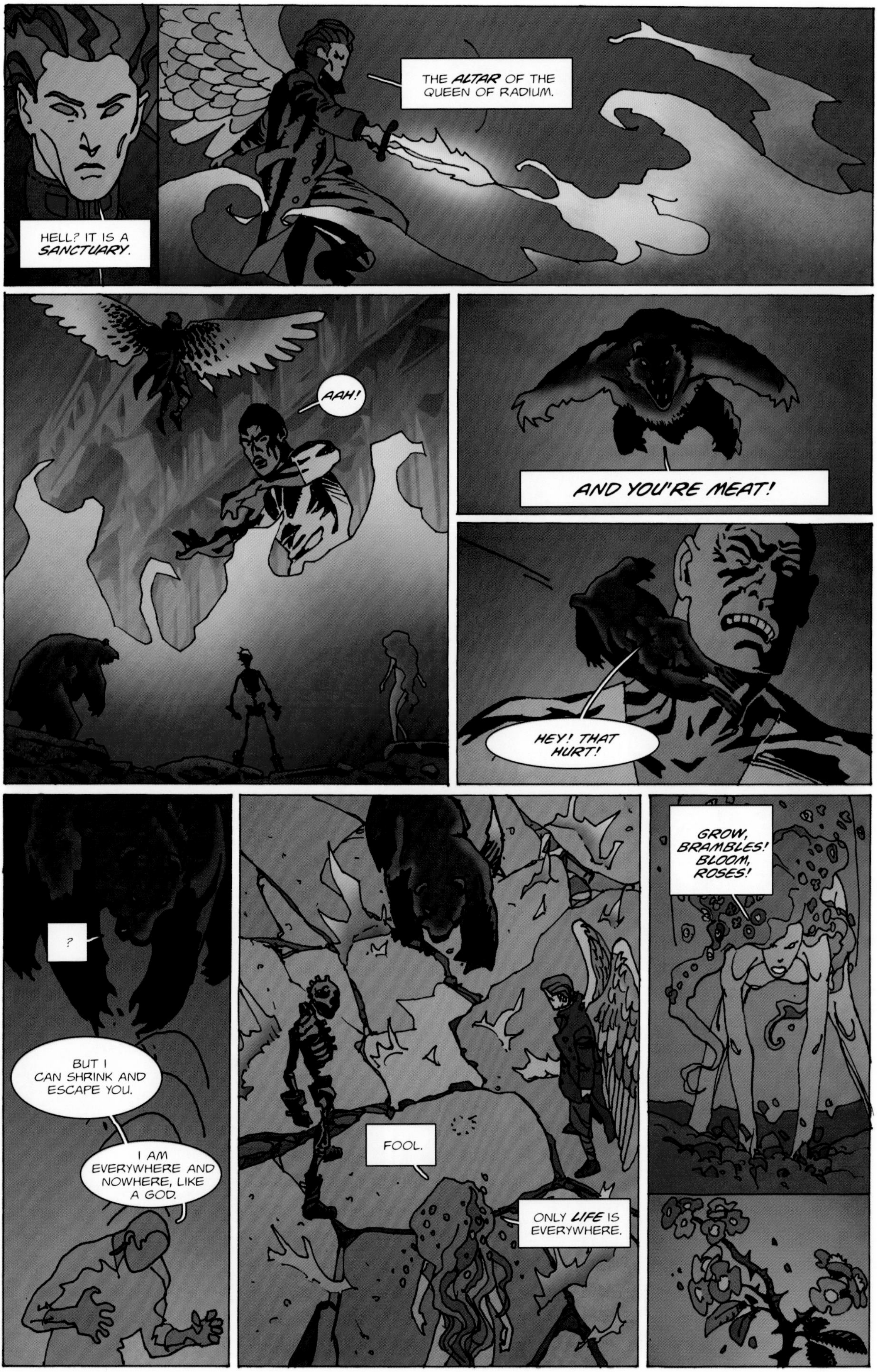
HELL? IT IS A SANCTUARY.
THE ALTAR OF THE QUEEN OF RADIUM.
AAH!
AND YOU'RE MEAT!
HEY! THAT HURT!
?
BUT I CAN SHRINK AND ESCAPE YOU.
I AM EVERYWHERE AND NOWHERE, LIKE A GOD.
FOOL.
ONLY LIFE IS EVERYWHERE.
GROW, BRAMBLES! BLOOM, ROSES!

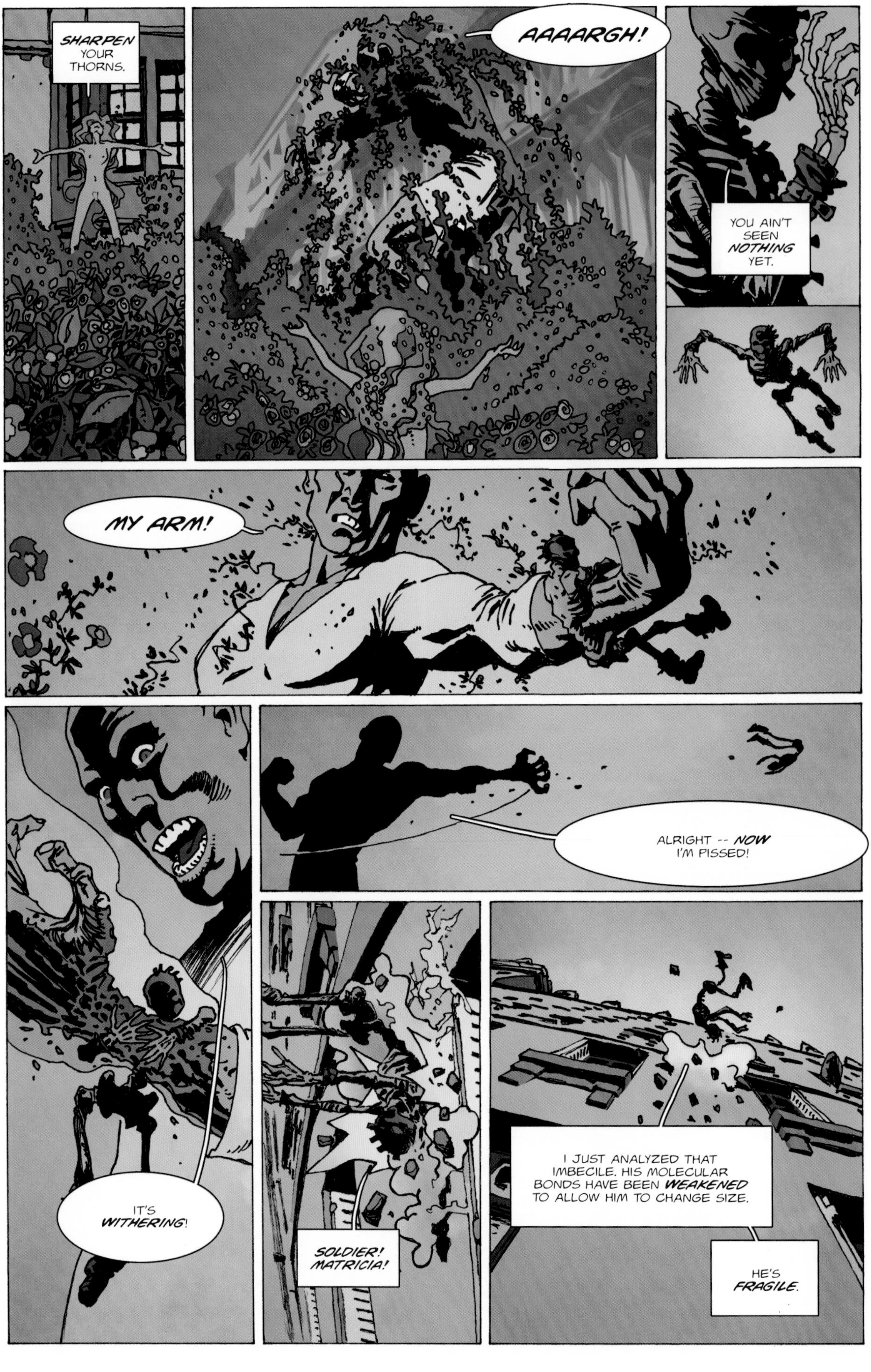
SHARPEN YOUR THORNS.
AAAARGH!
YOU AIN'T SEEN NOTHING YET.
MY ARM!
IT'S WITHERING!
ALRIGHT -- NOW I'M PISSED!
SOLDIER! MATRICIA!
I JUST ANALYZED THAT IMBECILE. HIS MOLECULAR BONDS HAVE BEEN WEAKENED TO ALLOW HIM TO CHANGE SIZE.
HE'S FRAGILE.

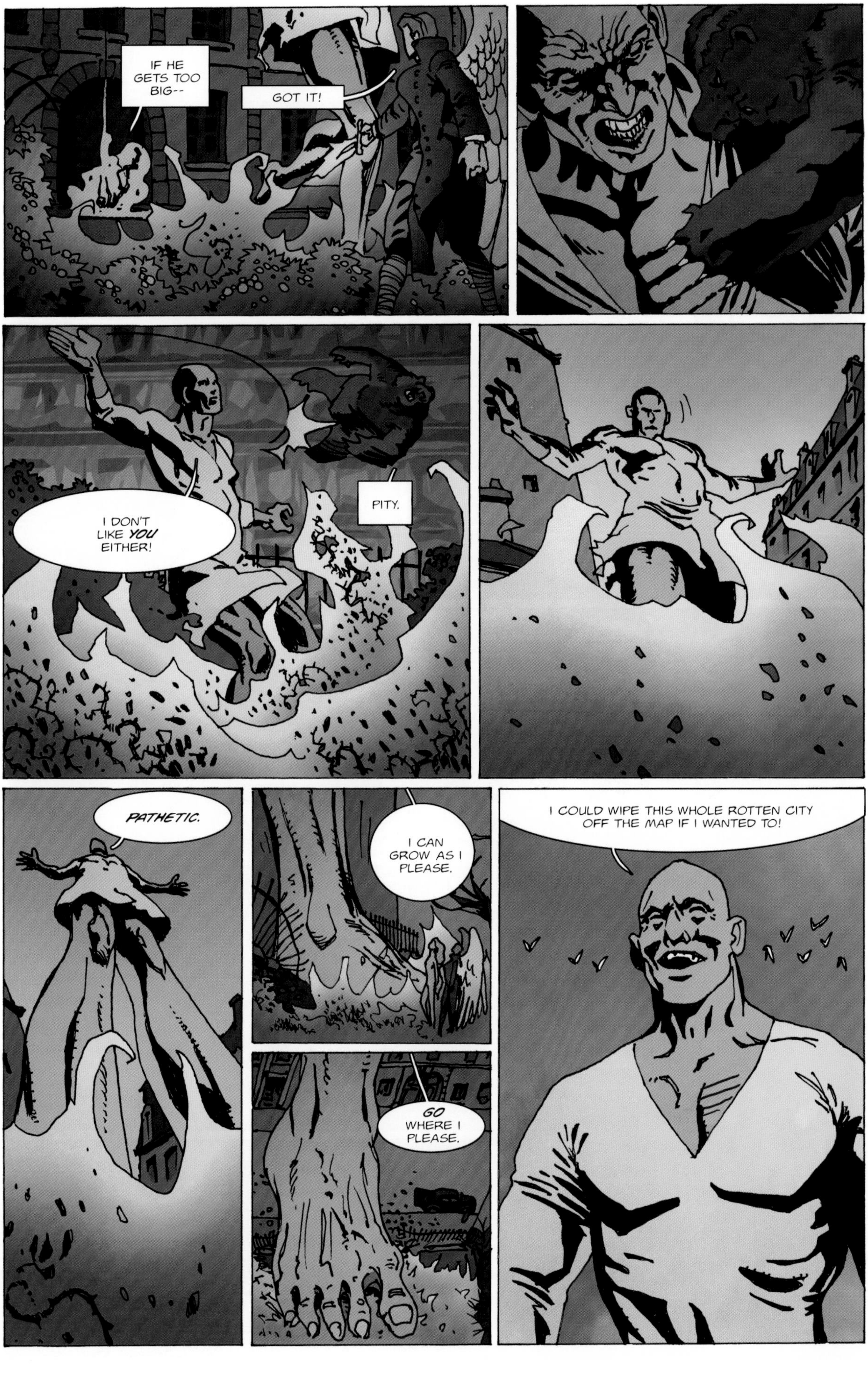
IF HE GETS TOO BIG--
GOT IT!
I DON'T LIKE YOU EITHER!
PITY.
PATHETIC.
I CAN GROW AS I PLEASE.
GO WHERE I PLEASE.
I COULD WIPE THIS WHOLE ROTTEN CITY OFF THE MAP IF I WANTED TO!

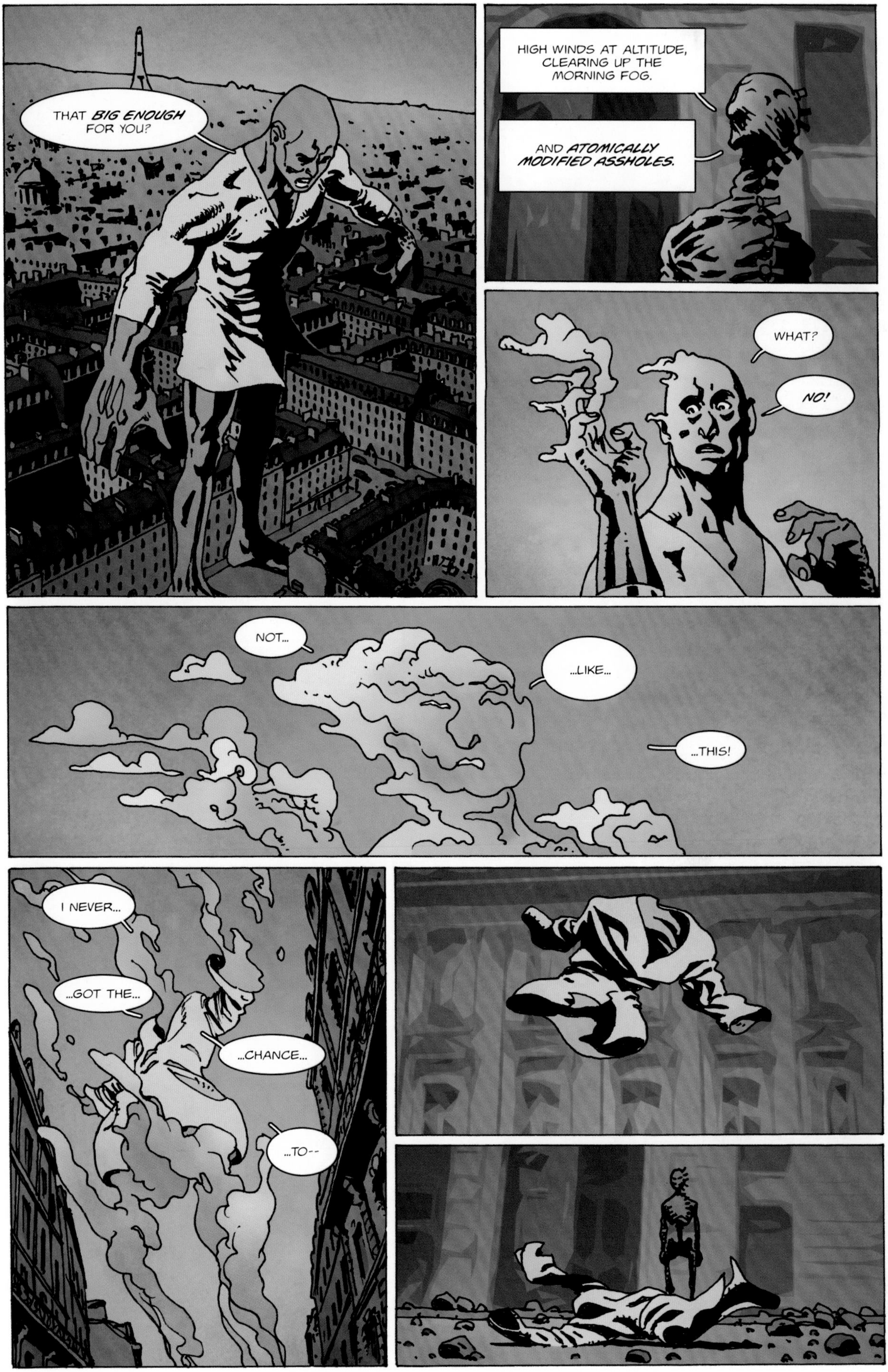
THAT BIG ENOUGH FOR YOU?
HIGH WINDS AT ALTITUDE, CLEARING UP THE MORNING FOG.
AND ATOMICALLY MODIFIED ASSHOLES.
WHAT?
NO!
NOT...
...LIKE...
...THIS!
I NEVER...
...GOT THE...
...CHANCE...
...TO--

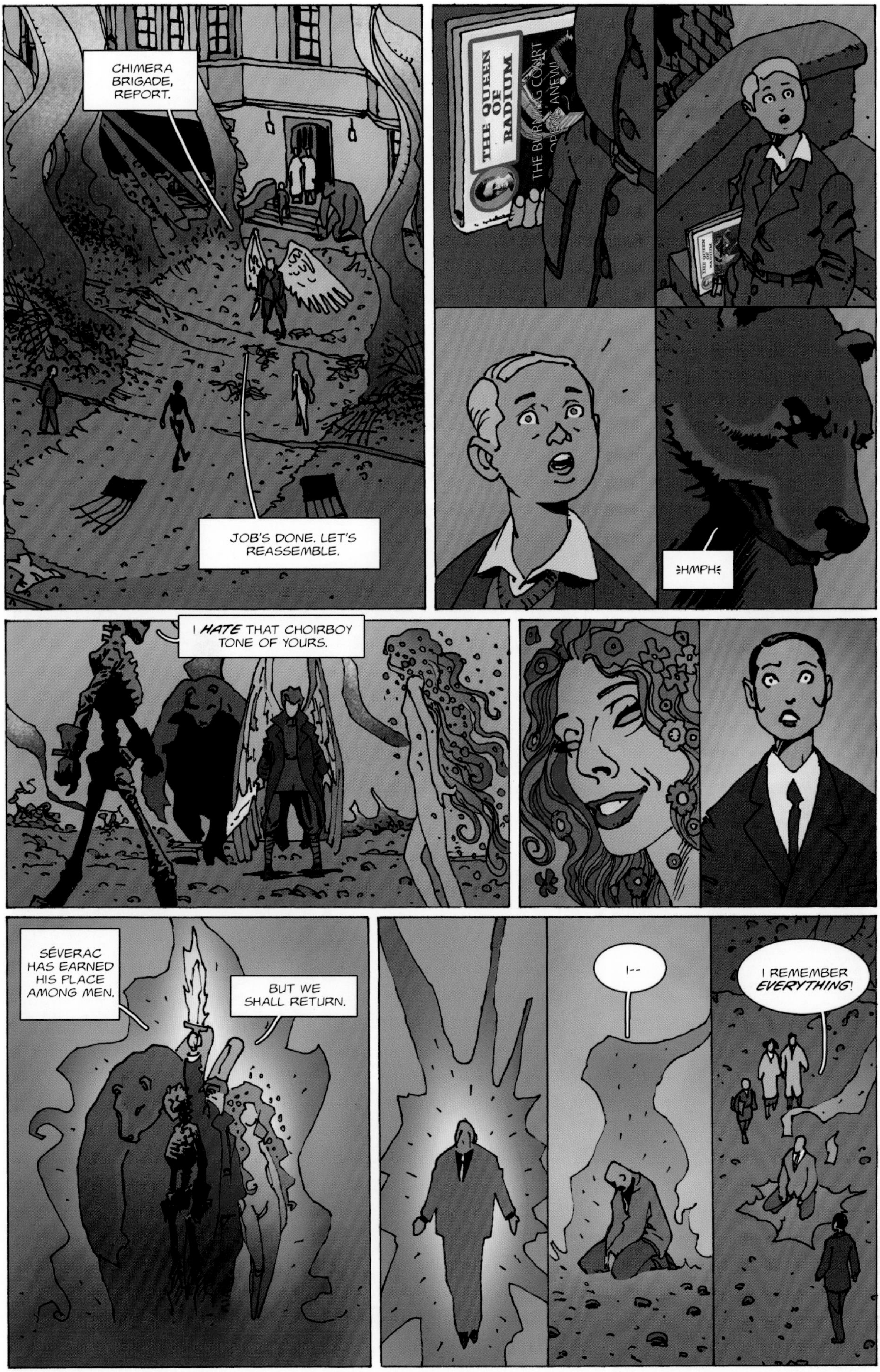
CHIMERA BRIGADE, REPORT.
JOB'S DONE. LET'S REASSEMBLE.
THE QUEEN OF RADIUM
THE BURNING COURT OPENS ANEW!
HMPH
I HATE THAT CHOIRBOY TONE OF YOURS.
SÉVERAC HAS EARNED HIS PLACE AMONG MEN.
BUT WE SHALL RETURN.
I--
I REMEMBER EVERYTHING!

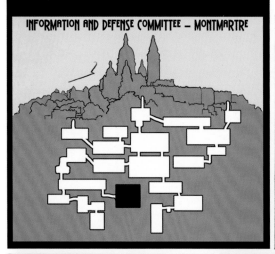

INFORMATION AND DEFENSE COMMITTEE – MONTMARTRE

SIR!

SIR!

OUR TEAM AT THE INSTITUTE JUST CALLED!

THE ELASTIC MAN'S ATTACK ON THE INSTITUTE FAILED, BUT--

LEAVE ME BE, CLAUDE. THAT'S NO LONGER IMPORTANT.

ANYWAY, THE C.I.D.'S ABOUT TO PROCEED WITH A LARGE-SCALE STRATEGY REVISION.

PARDON ME.

YOU WERE SAYING?

THAT YOU DID WELL TO CALL US.

SO ADMITTEDLY WE'VE HAD OUR DIFFERENCES IN THE PAST, BUT NOW -- FOR THE FIRST TIME -- WE HAVE A *COMMON INTEREST*. WE WISH TO KNOW WHAT DR. MISSBRAUCH IS UP TO IN CENTRAL EUROPE--

I *HAVE* THAT INFORMATION.

WHAT DO YOU OFFER IN EXCHANGE?

SOMETHING YOU *CANNOT* REFUSE.

NEXT EPISODE: THE BROKEN MAN!

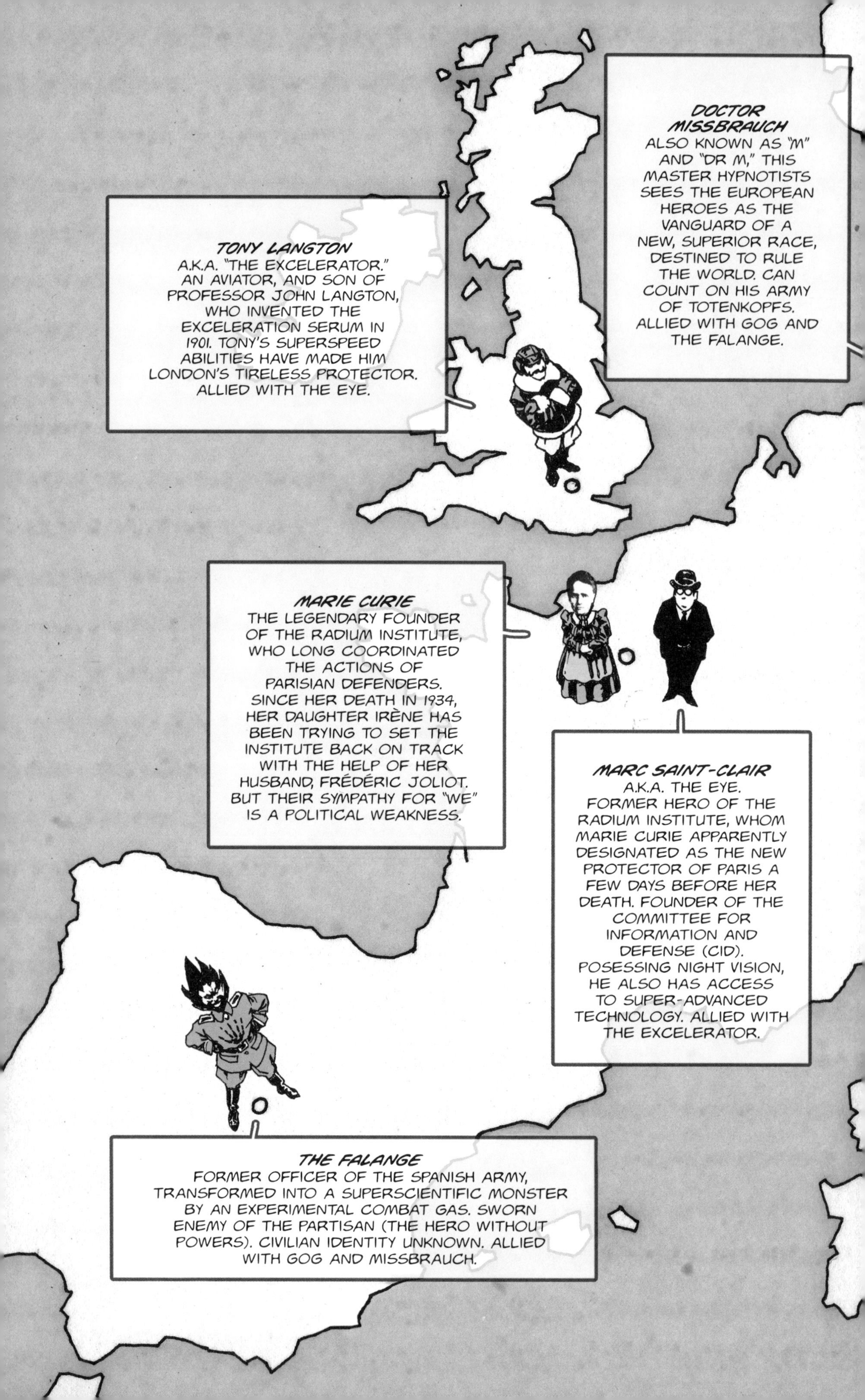
DOCTOR MISSBRAUCH
ALSO KNOWN AS "M" AND "DR M," THIS MASTER HYPNOTISTS SEES THE EUROPEAN HEROES AS THE VANGUARD OF A NEW, SUPERIOR RACE, DESTINED TO RULE THE WORLD. CAN COUNT ON HIS ARMY OF TOTENKOPFS. ALLIED WITH GOG AND THE FALANGE.
TONY LANGTON
A.K.A. "THE EXCELERATOR." AN AVIATOR, AND SON OF PROFESSOR JOHN LANGTON, WHO INVENTED THE EXCELERATION SERUM IN 1901. TONY'S SUPERSPEED ABILITIES HAVE MADE HIM LONDON'S TIRELESS PROTECTOR. ALLIED WITH THE EYE.
MARIE CURIE
THE LEGENDARY FOUNDER OF THE RADIUM INSTITUTE, WHO LONG COORDINATED THE ACTIONS OF PARISIAN DEFENDERS. SINCE HER DEATH IN 1934, HER DAUGHTER IRÈNE HAS BEEN TRYING TO SET THE INSTITUTE BACK ON TRACK WITH THE HELP OF HER HUSBAND, FRÉDÉRIC JOLIOT. BUT THEIR SYMPATHY FOR "WE" IS A POLITICAL WEAKNESS.
MARC SAINT-CLAIR
A.K.A. THE EYE. FORMER HERO OF THE RADIUM INSTITUTE, WHOM MARIE CURIE APPARENTLY DESIGNATED AS THE NEW PROTECTOR OF PARIS A FEW DAYS BEFORE HER DEATH. FOUNDER OF THE COMMITTEE FOR INFORMATION AND DEFENSE (CID). POSESSING NIGHT VISION, HE ALSO HAS ACCESS TO SUPER-ADVANCED TECHNOLOGY. ALLIED WITH THE EXCELERATOR.
THE FALANGE
FORMER OFFICER OF THE SPANISH ARMY, TRANSFORMED INTO A SUPERSCIENTIFIC MONSTER BY AN EXPERIMENTAL COMBAT GAS. SWORN ENEMY OF THE PARTISAN (THE HERO WITHOUT POWERS). CIVILIAN IDENTITY UNKNOWN. ALLIED WITH GOG AND MISSBRAUCH.